A River of Memories

A River of Memories

A Midwestern Boy
Lives Out His Dreams

GARY HINES

PUBLISHING + DESIGN

ISBN: 978-1-7345829-8-7

Library of Congress Control Number: 2021912447

Published in the United States of America by the Write Place,
Inc. For more information, please contact:

the Write Place, Inc.
809 W. 8th Street, Suite 2
Pella, Iowa 50219
www.thewriteplace.biz

Cover and interior design by Michelle Stam, the Write Place, Inc.
Cover photo by Gary Hines.
Author photo from personal collection.

The people and events described in this memoir are true and
represented to the best of my recollection. I offer my sincere
apology to anyone who may feel that the ensuing seventy years
have not allowed a more accurate portrayal. In a few cases,
names have been changed in the interest of privacy.

View other Write Place titles at thewriteplace.biz.

Dedication

For Borgie,
with gratitude for her profound influence on my life

Table of Contents

Foreword

As I entered my retirement, I looked around for what mattered to me now that I wasn't headed off to work every morning, as I had done for fifty years. In my unusual expanse of free time, my wife suggested writing about my (and our) early life. She felt our daughters knew so little about our backgrounds that an account would be interesting and helpful to them. Our oldest, Tara, knew a lot more because she had come along thirteen years earlier than her sisters. But our twins, Bretta and Jessie, knew little of our history.

So began this memoir. It is written as a "letter to my girls," and it begins, as we always taught them about telling stories, by starting at the beginning. They will remember our evening dinner table ritual of everybody having to "tell us about your day." When they resisted or had difficulty, I would always prompt them with, "Okay, I got up…"

It always did the trick.

Prologue

With my wife Jean's encouragement, I began to review childhood memories and plucked out some stories. But I found that at age seventy-five, grabbing memories out of the past is a lot like fishing. Just when you think you've got something, it slips away. Occasionally, you drag one in and savor the moment. Then whoosh … a flood of memories flows in like water down a rushing river.

Writing this book has given me the chance to relish each memory—and with still enough recall that I can share them.

1

Bright Glimpses of the Future

I sometimes joke that on the day I was born, the world took note by ending World War II. Official treaties were signed the next day, August 14, 1945. My mom recalled that they heard this news on the car radio on the way to the hospital. My dad said there was a big fire that day near our town of Ellsworth, Wisconsin, and that's why I was born with red hair.

My early life was truly wonderful. I didn't even know there were feelings other than total bliss. I think I was outside so much because we didn't have a TV. We also didn't have a phone, and my mom's directions were often, "Why don't you go outside?"

My dad was outside a lot too, mostly in the garage. He had quite a nice workbench in the basement (not exactly a "man cave," but pretty close). My dad … another whole book could be written about him. Nothing honors me more than when people draw comparisons between us, though I don't hold a candle.

When it was time for me to learn to drive—actually, well before it was time—he and I had a Saturday morning ritual of driving the trash to the city dump. Once he was behind the wheel, he would lift me onto his lap and let me do the steering. At about age twelve, he let me do the driving! I love driving to this day, and I credit it to my dad.

My dad was the most gentle, caring man you could imagine. He was a man of few words. Everything was always okay with him. He suffered grievously when my mom died after seventy years of marriage. On his deathbed, I remember when, only moments before his passing, I said to him, "It looks like you're going to be able to join Mom."

He replied, "Be okay."

2

Drawn to the Wilderness

The woods were a big part of my life, and my love of them persists today. I love the intrigue, the challenges, and the isolation from people. Even before I had my hunting bow and arrow or my beloved BB gun, the woods called to me. I could explore for hours, making paths, climbing trees (another passion), and flirting on the edge of getting lost. I went beyond the calling range of my mom or my older sister, Jeanine. At that time, the woods seemed endless. The sounds, delirious. Even today, there is no sound more enchanting than the distant cooing of mourning doves—that low, upward whistle, followed by one long coo and two short ones. *Uuu-ee-uuu, uu-uu…*

Eventually, I built a tree house. It was my first real solo construction, or project of any magnitude, and that milestone was significant and thrilling. I also built a soapbox (a cart for careening wildly down our gravel hill). My adult neighbor and mentor, Leroy, helped me a lot with the work. He also taught me how to make a real slingshot. I nailed quite a few birds with it (to the great disapproval of my grandmother, as they were her prized purple martins). They returned every year and lined up like an arcade range on the telephone line on the edge of her lawn. My best position was crouched in the lilac bushes, out of their sight. I am sure I loved that intoxicating smell of lilac then, as I do now, but I was never aware of it. All my focus was on the hunt.

The tree house was where I discovered how much I enjoyed being alone. Solitude—my secret, almost guilty, pleasure. Not even my friends, Cheryl and Steve, were invited there, nor my little sister, Janelle, who had just come along. I truly loved her. My *older* sister was the first girl in the family, but she was a mommy's girl and mommy's helper—which of course included helping her control that rambunctious little brother. Jeanine always delighted in repeating every order I got from mom … and, oh, how I loved ignoring them. She had no authority. (Although, as we were to learn, authority didn't carry a lot of weight with me).

About the same time as the woods and tree house era, the social me was starting to emerge. Little did I know how this side would come to rule my life. I made a lemonade stand out of a card table. Mom made the sugary-tart lemonade, and I set the stand up on the corner of our street. How I loved—okay, *craved*— the attention. Everyone in the neighborhood stopped by to visit, and I was the center of attention. Looking back now, it's easy to see this as my first "Corner Bar and Counseling Center," an idea that would serve my social needs far into my adult life.

Cars really didn't stop much, and there were no pedestrians. In those days, if you were walking, someone would always stop and give you a ride. And nobody ever said, "No, I'm just walking." That would have totally mystified the driver and certainly made for odd rumors in the neighborhood. My local friends came by the stand, but they never had any money. I wasn't set up for credit cards, as they didn't exist for another twenty years. I'm sure I just gave them the lemonade—a business model that unfortunately stuck with me.

I prayed every night in those days, on my knees by my bed. I especially prayed whenever I wanted something really badly. It sometimes worked. My dad also prayed every night by his bed—and did so until his death at ninety-six. He was a faithful Catholic and the one who taught me to pray. My mom knelt by the bed each night as well, right across from him, but I think her thoughts were more on bridge club. She was Lutheran after all.

Praying, as Dad taught me well, often did pay off. He knew I was praying for that first bike and voilà—a bike! Dad was one religious guy, and he had his wires tuned with God. Even if he had to play a small intermediary role, he made sure the value of prayer sunk in with me. It certainly did with my sisters, perhaps to this day. But I needed the full treatment, not just church on Sunday (High Mass, where I was an altar boy and later a trainer of altar boys). We also attended Saturday evening service or Low Mass, which was mercifully shorter. Thursday night was confession, where I got my money's worth. That was in addition to the all-day, every-day Catholic school taught (and ruled) by nuns. Ruled … as in with a ruler! I remember once after misbehaving at recess, a nun lined a few of us boys up against the wall, our backs to the blackboard. She had us hold our hands out, palms down. Then she severely whacked each of our hands with the ruler, just like in the movies. (Today, Jean keeps a yardstick.)

At night, I was especially restless. There was life out there, teeming with people and all manner of interesting nighttime activities that I was missing out on. I had to go see it. So once my parents and sisters were asleep, I'd slip out the back door and walk across the field, through a small woods, and down the hill to where I was level with the tops of buildings. I discovered I could easily jump onto the roof of the Coca-Cola bottling building. Here I found my perfect spot to sit and take it all in.

There were nine bars in East Ellsworth. I remember thinking that if the entire population (about nine hundred people) needed to, they could fit in the bars. There'd be about a hundred in each. I never saw any big fights or shoot-outs, but watching people meandering around in the wee hours fascinated me.

Eventually, either simply tired or fearing I'd be discovered missing, I'd head back home. Getting back into the house could be a little tricky, as I had to get to my upstairs bedroom. I couldn't go in the first-floor door, as I'd have to pass my parents' bedroom.

Fortunately, I had a *conspirator*. Janelle was always ready to help her big brother with his shenanigans, and she would help me crawl through the window of her first-floor bedroom.

Then I could sneak upstairs to my room. She risked the wrath of not only Mom and Dad, but even more so our big sister. Don't try this stunt with Jeanine.

During this time, I had my first actual job (not counting my paper route, which was more a rite of passage). The job was candling eggs, which was the process used to determine if eggs were developing correctly. In the incubation stage, an egg should be mostly opaque, with a dark spot indicating the embryo. I'd hold each egg to a bright light and examine it. Bad eggs can be easily detected by a trained candler (like me!) and removed as the eggs pass by on a conveyor. Now the process is automated, but back then it was simple employment for anyone. I remember I was paid, not by the hour but by the egg! And it wasn't much.

The term "bad egg"—as in "that kid is a bad egg"—came from this process. And yes, it may have been applied to me once or twice.

3

The Root Beer Stand

In my early teens, something fantastic occurred, a major milestone in my young life: My dad bought me a root beer stand. This was no toy, but a full-blown, adult-run business that served the community, as well as anyone on the busy highway through our end of town.

It was a wooden structure, about ten feet square, that had been built and run for years by an older couple. Dad heard they were ready to retire, and he purchased it without my knowledge. He paid eight hundred dollars and bought it only for me. He had no intention of working there, nor did my mom or my sisters. My parents both had full-time jobs and saw the root beer stand as something to keep me out of trouble, as they saw some small signs of me heading in that direction. My sisters might have said *big signs*. They would point to incidents like the night I broke into the root beer stand. I was just out roaming in the middle of the night, as I loved to do, and I didn't have the key. But that didn't stop me. However, the police took notice, picked me up, and took me home to my once more dismayed parents.

My ever-social soul took to this little enterprise like a fish to water. Oh, I loved it! And it was a true business, little as it was. The entrance was a door on the back. The other three sides all had heavy, fold-up wooden windows. The windows could be latched to a big hook, revealing a serving counter underneath. The grand centerpiece was a big, round wooden barrel—the root beer barrel, of course. There was a big spout on the front, with a large lever that served as a faucet; you turned the lever to the left to fill the frosty mug. You turned it to the right for the last quarter of the pour, to create the foamy head. We kept the mugs in a long freezer that also held ice cream and frozen treats. The root beer was sold in a standard sized glass mug. It was five cents for a regular and ten cents for a large, and we sold a ton. The taste was truly delicious—a blend of nutty and sweet, not the sweetness of other pop, but a more bold and adult taste. My love of this refreshing drink may well have foreshadowed my affection for a similar adult beverage today. Friends today can quickly see that this was the second incarnation of the Corner Bar and Counseling Center.

Surprisingly for such a tiny operation, we also sold lots of food—hot dogs and two varieties of hot beef sandwiches (a BBQ one and a shredded beef one). The meat came in large cans that we simply emptied into heaters. They were delicious, enhanced by being served on hot buns fresh from a local bakery and kept in a steamer. We also sold popcorn that was displayed in a clear, lighted plastic machine. It had a big serving outlet and looked like a real popcorn popper. (In truth, it just warmed the popcorn, which came in giant bags from a food wholesaler.)

That popcorn machine resides in my garage—today's Corner Bar and Counseling Center—and it is regularly filled for my happy neighbors. It is one of the highlights of my annual Oktoberfest, where it's fun to tell of the machine's age and legacy.

At the root beer stand, we also sold ice cream cones (a regular for five cents, and a heaped-up one for ten cents). The place was busy most of the day and super busy in the evening. In general, people sat in their cars, and we went out, took their orders, and served them on an aluminum tray that rested on their car window. Eventually, I had carhops in the evening. One was quite a cute girl, who I will always remember. (Girls, another youthful obsession of mine, had no *off* position! I had entered high school, and of course the hormones were raging, and it was heaven.)

During the school year, the root beer stand was open in the evenings and on weekends. That didn't leave me a lot of free time, but it served my socializing needs perfectly. Kids liked to hang out, girls included, and I was popular as the proprietor. I also had my new best friend, Bill, who was a year ahead of me in school. One of the more famous episodes of our friendship—and a telling one—took place during high school homecoming. There was a traditional bonfire and a large crowd of kids. A rumor was circulating that my long-standing feud with some of the "tough guys" was coming to a head, and I was going to fight one nemesis in particular, Kenny. The feud was over my relationship with a girl, of course—in this case, his sister. (I had only dated her once, which for me was like ignoring her!)

And so the confrontation came to pass as foretold, with me enduring a well-attended fight with the tough Kenny. Ironically, *I won the fight*—but then I got beat up by his much larger friend later that night (also a well-attended event). This fight was a classic, rolling into the street and so forth. Fight number one had been more of a boxing match in a big circle of kids, with not a lot of damage done; number two was in the middle of downtown, outside the major hangout (Charlie's Soda Fountain), and it was a serious brawl. This one I did not win, following which good old Bill literally scraped me off the street and hauled me home, not just defeated but pretty banged up. Fortunately, Bill was bigger and nobody messed with him. I believe this was the night my folks decided they should look into a private school (or if they were already thinking along these lines, it was the evidence they needed). I knew my days in the old hometown were numbered. Private school would be a good move for me, but of course it proved a complete failure in correcting the behavior that prompted it.

4

High School Success

After the root beer stand, my next employment was working in a ladies' clothing store.

My beloved grandfather—Tony, or "Poppy" to us kids—owned and operated what at the time was the only grocery store in East Ellsworth. He and my grandmother—Dora, or "Nanny"—had moved to Ellsworth from the old family farm east of town. My mother, Lolah, worked in her father's store, and one of her duties was taking the day's cash down the street a few doors to the bank, where my father was the teller. Need I say more? Perfect fate. They met, fell in love, married, and built a house up on the hill.

As it was senseless to take out the car for a mere couple of miles, my dad walked to work every day. Of course, walking (for the purpose of getting someplace) was common then. I walked to school every day, about a mile each way.

When Poppy could no longer handle the rigors of the grocery business, my mother and her mother took over the store and converted it into a ladies' dress shop. Dora & Lola's Style Shop was known for miles around. (Incidentally, "Dora & Lola's" is not a typo—they thought Lola was a snazzier name than Lolah, especially when used with Dora!) I worked there for a few years, as did Janelle. I was still running the root beer stand then, but my mornings were free, so I would sit a few hours in the basement to work on the store's bookkeeping. I would often accompany my mother on trips to the warehouse district in Minneapolis, where she would buy inventory for the store (mostly dresses, which she sold for as low as $2.99). The store also carried a small stock of "better" dresses, intended for a few select ladies (often reserved for them by name … especially Dora and Lolah). And they carried a variety of the "unmentionable" garments, of which the women in those days wore plenty. As the only clothing store in Ellsworth, it was quite a thriving enterprise.

Meanwhile, at Ellsworth High, I was cruising along fine. I was in the German and Theater Clubs, and I had a small part in a school play. That led to another discovery that played a big role in my life for years to come: I enjoyed performing for groups. Being in the Theater Club introduced me to a new skill called "memorized declamation." It was another of those "like a fish to water" moments. Never any good at sports, here was something at which I might excel.

In my sophomore year speech class, I decided to perform "Thanatopsis" by William Cullen Bryant. It is a long and complex poem about life and death, especially renowned for its use of imagery and syntax and written when the poet was nineteen years old. Read aloud, it is remarkably moving. I got pretty good at it, earning top honors and a trip to Madison for the speech state finals, where I also won top honors. Here are some of the best lines:

> *"Yet not to thine eternal resting-place*
> *Shalt though retire alone, nor couldst thou wish*
> *Couch more magnificent. Thou shalt lie down*
> *With patriarchs of the infant world—with kings,*
> *The powerful of the earth—the wise, the good*
> *Fair forms and hoary seers of ages past..."*

The next year I remained in speech. For my competition in memorized declamation, I chose "A Piece of String," a short story by French author Guy de Maupassant. It's the story of an old man who bends to pick up a small piece of string in the street. A rumor starts that he picked up a *handbag*, missing at the time and said to contain five hundred francs. The more he protests his innocence, the less he is believed. The story is sometimes cited for illustrating the theory that once you are accused of something, even when later found innocent, you will always be thought of as guilty in the eyes of some.

Here is an excerpt from the story:

> *"He began anew to tell his tale, lengthening his*
> *recital every day, each day adding new proofs, more*

energetic declarations and more sacred oaths, which he thought of, which he prepared in his hours of solitude, for his mind was entirely occupied with the story of the string. The more he denied it, the more artful his arguments, the less he was believed."

Once again, I won top honors and a trip to state.

Like most young guys (perhaps a little more), girls had also come to play a major role in my evolving world. With little interest in school, sports, or cars, my focus became consumed with a string of young romances.

STREET SCENE - EAST ELLSWORTH - WIS

Courtesy of the Pierce County Historical Association.

5

Leaving Small-Town Life

It amazes me to this day that my parents—not individuals of the worldly elite—were working on a scheme to rescue my misdirected life. I'd had a few fights, which was common those days, and school didn't really get my attention. Schoolwork was easy, but "he does not work up to his ability" was the common refrain. Junior year was to be my last at the public high school. The train to my next milestone had left the station. My new home would be St. John's Preparatory—an expensive, *all boys* private boarding school in the north woods. Wowzer! This was *not* Ellsworth High.

The idea of leaving town for private school presented a big dilemma. It sounded intriguing, but I was also having a pretty good time at home (the occasional fistfight notwithstanding). Rock music was coming onto the airwaves, and we had it blasting nonstop at the root beer stand. It was talking directly to us, and the song "Sweet Little Suzie" said it all. In 1959, every teenager was "going with" somebody. Some of the matchups switched around from time to time, but nobody who was anybody stayed single very long. In my early high school days, I was with Judy; we'd stayed together as we made the move from Catholic grade school to the much larger public high school. But with the larger school came a much larger pool of girls, and my antenna flew around like a twig in a hurricane. Before long, I had zeroed in on my choice—lo and behold, another Judy.

New Judy was a farm girl, and she was just as cute as the dickens. She was the lead band majorette. She was a baton-twirling, short-skirted spectacle that sent my heart racing. Those white marching boots, those strong, farm-girl legs, that ultra-short skirt … all was paraded (literally) in front of me like water before a dying man. I was a total goner, dreaming of having her with me.

Without any ceremony that I remember, New Judy and I became a couple. This was the real thing—we knew it. Forever, for absolute sure. It was sophomore year for me, freshman for her. We attended junior prom together. She was gorgeous in the pale blue dress she had made. Later, we parked along the road to her farmhouse. I had my first experiences of any *touching* with a girl—and at *her* invitation. It all but disoriented me. To this day, our 1962 prom theme of "Moon River" stirs my heart. (Fittingly, "Moon River" won the Academy Award for Best Original Song that year. I agreed completely, although it was sung by Audrey Hepburn in the movie *Breakfast at Tiffany's*.)

The next year, Judy and I repeated it all. By then I had moved to St. John's Preparatory, and I wasn't shy about displaying the new me—I recall I wore a brand-new madras shirt to prom. Certainly unheard of at Ellsworth High, madras is a material with multiple faint colors arranged in a striped-plaid design. It originated in India and has some religious association. Wearing a large madras shirt *untucked* was the thing in my new private school circles. Wearing it to the EHS prom sent a blaring signal to everyone there in their stuffy suits and ties.

That Gary Hines sure looks weird.

Funny that I didn't get in any fights that night. As to the after-hours of prom, we'd become Olympic caliber at *necking*, another activity I fully embraced. But by junior year, some scattered clouds were circling for Judy and me, since the private school world had introduced me to a whole new category of girls.

Courtesy of Br. Paul-Vincent Niebauer, OSB, St. John's Abbey.

6

St. John's Prep School

Talk about a place I didn't belong. Because of my disregard for authority, the discipline of prep school was excruciating for me. We had mass at 7:00 a.m. every day, after communal showers, and we were commanded to bed at 9:00 p.m., with lights out. I managed the routine fairly well. Even as a newcomer to the class of around fifty, I eventually made friends. But the academics were another story.

These guys were absolutely light-years ahead of me. At home, I was easily in the top ten percent (even without "working up to my ability"). At this classy place, I graduated forty-ninth out of a class of fifty—and fiftieth was a disaster who was kicked out of school just before graduation. I was one of the few who liked him and even took him home with me one weekend. We double-dated, with Judy and a friend she rounded up for him. It really did not go well. He was kind of a troubled kid, just part of the cast I'd picked up on my journey away from Ellsworth. His expulsion freed up the bottom place.

However, at St. John's my future was bursting open like a warm spring day. There were fascinating new friends I was eager to know, despite being a poor—and poorly educated—small-town kid. It was a true challenge, being thrown among a band of well-educated, rich, and elite young guys. Even as a fairly social and personable guy, it was an uphill battle. I'm sure it would've helped if I had been an athlete, or had anything else whatsoever to offer. I enjoyed a little fleeting fame from my conversant ability in German, which was studied in all Wisconsin high schools in those days. But with this school being steeped in the academic traditions, it was taught as an academic subject, essentially removed from any social or conversational context. These guys could diagram a sentence; I could tell a story.

I have a picture from my last year at Ellsworth High, showing the German Club playing pool in the bedroom of my old house. My dear Poppy had purchased it for me, and he loved to play pool himself. Around a pool table today, I'm still drawn to his pool quips. "Hit'm where they shine" (an actual pool tactic).

I look at that picture and I know we were all speaking German—fluently, casually. Among my elite prep school colleagues, I had that one calling card!

There was a memorable day in German class at St. John's. I cannot remember the teacher's name (which is kind of telling, as I still remember that the high school German teacher in Ellsworth was Mr. Beyer). Anyway, the question was: "When do words receive an umlaut?" (That's the two little dots over a vowel that change its pronunciation.) I knew instinctively when umlauts were used and was entirely comfortable with that element in the language, but I had no idea what the *rule* was. Of course, I got called on to answer this question of grammatical rule. At a total loss, I wise-cracked, "When in doubt, umlaut."

I owned the room. Everybody cracked up, including the teacher—my calling card had been put to perfect use.

I was trying to fit in and make friends, and I had one small but oh-so-critical success. I had begun talking just a bit with John, a pleasant but very studious guy who wore black -rimmed glasses. We were not much alike (in fact, hardly at all). But somehow we jelled and were destined to become best friends for the rest of our lives.

When we had just enough of a budding friendship, we shared a ride back home for a weekend. There were only a few home weekends, and they were prized. His father drove up to the school alone to pick us up, as John's mother had passed away when John was about fifteen. It was now 1962, and his mother had died in 1961. I remember considering John to be somewhat of a quiet lad, and I wonder now how his temperament may have been shaped by this loss. In a curious twist, his little sister, Sue, would eventually become my closest female friend.

John's dad was a lawyer, like many of the boys' fathers. The rest were doctors. I allowed that *my dad* was a banker (skipping the detail that he was a teller and also the janitor). Anyway, John's father was coming to pick him up for the weekend. We figured we could get back home, where we both had access to cars, and we'd play the weekend by ear. In fact, we ended up a trio, as his good friend Rich had already been planning to go with John. Rich had a steady girlfriend in Minneapolis who attended the equally prestigious Holy Angels Academy. Her name was Penny. I had Judy to get back to.

Courtesy of Susan Halloran.

7

Heading to California

My next significant move was to get kicked out of St. John's University. I had enrolled there, as was the natural progression for most prep school students. Although not *entirely* natural for the kid at the bottom of the class, still hopelessly unable to heed the continuing drumbeat of "does not work up to his ability." Getting accepted at St. John's required a trip up to the school with my parents for a somber sit-down with the high priest, mainly because I was the bottom-of-the-class kid. The visit went well, as I was sincere and contrite and expressed a willingness to finally apply myself (this performance was perhaps in line with a major in theater). And it worked. There I was, enrolled at St. John's University, among the best colleges in the country.

I lasted about two months. Talk about a place I didn't belong! Devoutly religious. Demandingly academic. No girls. Not really a great fit. Another kid from the prep school, Wayne, was in about the same shape as me. He was so incredibly smart that he made the grade okay without applying himself, but his behavioral antics were a giant problem. I really enjoyed him and, unfortunately I also learned from him. He was one very wild guy, and I can now appreciate that I viewed him as a role model. Also, it was a big plus that girls adored him—a fact of which he was entirely aware. So Wayne and I blew out of St. John's together. He went to nearby St. Cloud one day and came back with a 1957 Chevy. We packed up and took off—headed for California!

We made it as far as Des Moines, Iowa. Broke and down-trodden, we had no choice but to stop to look for a place to stay and a way to make money.

Unsurprisingly, Wayne found both things for us. The guy could charm his way out of Auschwitz! We had a basement apartment—it's the only place I've ever lived in with an actual dirt floor. We were both employed as door-to-door salesmen for a pots and pans company. He did pretty well, Mr. Charm, but I never sold a single item. I didn't try much either. Despite all my extroversion, I just didn't feel like it. We were literally poor and hungry, and before long I ended up in the hospital, suffering from malnutrition and mononucleosis. My parents soon arrived, rescuing their wayward son one more time. By this time, I'm sure they wished they'd had three girls.

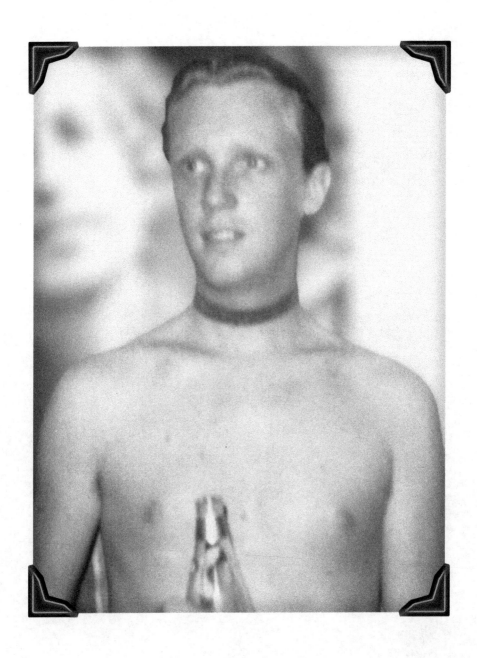

8

My Love Affair with the Military

Back home in Wisconsin, I was still the restless, undisciplined, anti-authority young fellow. What could be a better fit for me than the U.S. military? My friend, good old Billy, had a brainstorm: *Why don't we go into the Army?*

For me, the Army was another brutal wake up into adulthood. The misfit was exposed almost immediately. I remember one afternoon, early in this dreadful experience, when our squad was in full platoon formation. We were going through our drill exercises with shouted commands.

"Right shoulder, arms."

"Forward, march."

Then the command came: "Left face, *sequential.*"

The drill instructor expected us to face sharply to the left *at the same time.* The word he should have used, of course, was *simultaneous.* I pointed this out to him.

Army drill sergeants are not a breed particularly open to criticism. I felt his eyes piercing into me. I had just earned myself a trip out behind the barracks for a clear lesson about this rule.

Following boot camp for National Guard soldiers was six years of monthly weekend duty. On one of these "weekend warriors" adventures, while I was living in Prescott, I had brief access to a storage room for rocket-propelled grenades. They were just sitting there … so, naturally, I took one. They were about two feet long and eight inches around, and they weighed maybe ten pounds. These were "training rockets," so they didn't contain the final explosive, but they did have a huge amount of incendiary material that would propel the device to its target miles away. Anyway, I threw one onto the back seat of my car.

After a few days driving around with this thing resting peacefully in the back of my Pontiac, I decided to do something with it. With all the caution and good judgment for which I was known, I drove a mile or two out of town and parked on the side of the road. It was a rural, wooded area; I grabbed the rocket and carried it to what I figured was a suitable clearing. Not wanting to send the rocket streaming into the skies over Prescott, I buried it nose-down and went about determining how it could be detonated. *What was there to worry about? It couldn't reach China!*

Finally, I gathered a few handfuls of dry leaves and twigs, shaping them into a little pile on the up-facing rear of the device. Seemed pretty safe to me, so I started the little pile on fire, ran full speed to my car, and took off like a bandit. I watched in the rearview mirror as a gigantic, billowing plume of white smoke shot into the air.

Thrilling!

I drove on a little farther—trembling, I admit—then turned and headed back toward Prescott. On the way, I was met by two firetrucks and a police car heading out for whatever the hell *that* was!

Yes, the Army and I certainly did not belong together. On another occasion, during my brief tenure with the National Guard, I was attached to a float bridge company that operated out of Ellsworth. Their weekend duty was loading up the bridge materials, driving to the Mississippi River near Red Wing, and building a bridge. We'd complete it to the point that our trucks could drive over it, then disassemble it, re-load it, and return home. During one of these useless exercises, I snuck off to a spot along the river where it was rumored you could find marijuana growing. Well, I found some, picked a small bundle, and hid it in one of the Army trucks. Arriving back at our base, I stuffed it into the trunk of my car.

We were unfamiliar with marijuana at the time. By this point, a friend and I were living in an apartment above an old house near downtown Minneapolis. We hung the stuff in the kitchen to dry, eventually deciding to dry it in the oven. This did the job, so we crumpled some up into a joint and tried smoking it. Nothing. Just a very nasty cough and a sore throat.

Well, chalk up another stupid thing I had to try.

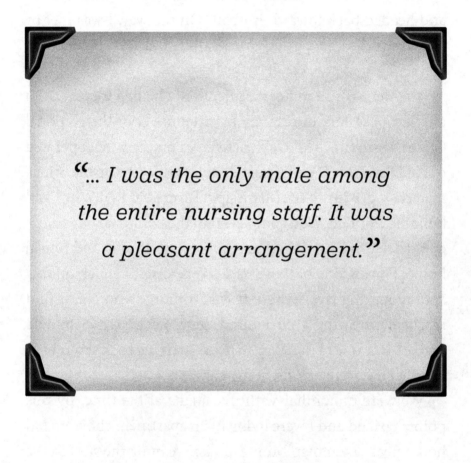

"*... I was the only male among the entire nursing staff. It was a pleasant arrangement.*"

9

Life in a Mental Hospital

Following my failed excursion to California with Wayne—and my parents' rescue—I resumed life back in Wisconsin. I joined the National Guard, and my dad also arranged a job for me at a hospital that was owned by the same man who owned the bank where Dad had worked nearly all his adult life. The hospital was actually a mental institution, and my job as an orderly provided my living quarters. I became a resident of St. Croixdale in Prescott, Wisconsin—a town that would provide the base and launching pad for my adventurous next phase. I loved the job, the staff, the residents, the pay, the free food, the lodging, and the freedom. Moreover, the job exposed me to elements of life that were entirely foreign, and they made deep impressions.

This was the mid-sixties, and my job included distributing medicine, doing intrusive enemas, administering hypodermic shots, and holding people down for their electroconvulsive shock treatments. Dressed all in white, I felt like a real health-care professional. I was so proud of my skill at giving shots that I did a demonstration on the technique for a class at college. I came to the front of the classroom and gave myself an injection in the shoulder with sterilized water.

But just below that spiffy, clean persona lurked my darker side, with a supply of hormones that could serve a small army. In addition to the main hospital building, which housed most of the patients, there were a few surrounding cottages for less worrisome patients, each with two or three bedrooms. My home was a bedroom in one of those cottages, and I was the only male among the entire nursing staff. It was a pleasant arrangement.

I soon re-enrolled in school, with my folks paying tuition (they did not give up easily). This time I was at River Falls State College, a few miles away. I'd again been supplied a car (a giant 1959 Pontiac, which had been purchased for me, totally out of the blue, by my older sister). I split my time between classes and hours at the hospital.

Young people can be so oblivious, and I was no different. Here I was, living in a mental hospital, with folks who were seriously disabled … and I was *befriending* them.

One of the patients, Kevin, was only a little older than me and classically schizophrenic. He talked constantly to someone who was not there; he giggled continuously, despite trying to stifle it, and he gestured madly with his hands as he stared into the distance. He was also taking college classes. Every day, I gave him a ride to and from school, and he never seemed to have any self-conscious concern about his behavior.

Another St. Croixdale patient, Fred, also became a friend. Fred couldn't speak and was bed-bound, but he had the biggest smile on earth, and he could listen. Mentally, he was fine—he was keenly interested in my dating exploits and would spastically wave his hands to show his desire to hear more. I would spend a lot of time sitting at Fred's bedside. I liked the guy a lot and enjoyed being with him … and I was there at his bedside when he passed away.

10

The Girl Next Door

My life in Prescott came at a time when I was passing milestones like exits on a freeway ... and one exit I couldn't pass up was called *Mary*.

I was working at the hospital one day when some papers needed to be delivered to the hospital owner, Mr. McGrath. His house was only a few blocks away, so I walked over. The house was huge—all white with giant pillars in the front, sort of like the famous house in D.C. On a small-town street, it looked like a mansion. Mr. McGrath's neighbors across the street lived in a more modest home, and they had a daughter about my age. As I approached the house, she happened to be outside. Always ready for a new friend, especially an attractive young woman, I introduced myself.

Mary had a porcelain doll appearance—very pretty, with starkly white skin and dark hair. But the "fragile doll" part only extended to her appearance. She was friendly, lively, and eager to talk. We talked, hit it off, and began dating. She and her family were devoutly Catholic, and it was worrisome for her to be suddenly dating this guy who worked at the nearby mental hospital (and always brought her home quite late). I learned later they had even spoken to their local priest about it. The relationship was doomed from the start, however. Life up at St. John's had introduced me to a whole new category of girls.

Courtesy of Janelle Hill.

11

Private School Girls

We're going to return to my prep school days for a moment. I want to introduce Penny, who attended Holy Angels. She was one of those classy, sarcastic, spicy-mouthed, Ferlinghetti-loving, private school phenomena who were totally new to me. Until then, most girls I'd known sat primly with their knees carefully together. Penny slouched, usually with one leg over the arm of a chair, seemingly unaware of where her skirt was. I wonder now if her all-girls school life had created such unconscious displays.

The first time I met Penny, she was attending St. Benedict's, the all-girls counterpart down the road from St. John's University. She was the girlfriend of a college freshman at St. John's, a guy who was known to my friend John from his prep school days. The setting was her boyfriend's dorm room at the university, and the whole thing was a bit dreamlike for me. I'd never been in a college dorm room, and Penny's boyfriend struck me as a rock star. He was good-looking, confident, and played the guitar. Rich, my new friend from St. John's Prep, was there too. Neither of us could keep our eyes off Penny. Her short skirt and long blonde hair were like a flashing billboard to us, but it was her personality that really made her irresistible. Penny was at once cute and funny and a little profane—a new combination for me to digest.

We all sat around and chatted, listening to the guitar—like any bunch of carefree, good-looking, rich kids at a private school. Except that I was really not a contender. As the world would turn, Rich was next in line. He had the looks, personality, and desire to step into Penny's world, and he soon did. The coupling and re-coupling continued, however, and Rich—ever the Don Juan—soon had his sights on still *another* prize (much more about her to come). I edged cautiously toward Penny, surprised to find little resistance.

So began one of the dearest in my chain of young romances. I was crazy about Penny, and it felt more like love than anything had yet. We frequently double-dated with John, who continued to find new girls for himself. He and everyone loved Penny and approved. (It's fair to say that Billy *actually* loved her!) There was one notable exception: her mother. Penny's mom was a char- acter—wealthy, eccentric, bitchy. For some reason, she liked John and treated him most graciously. She was not the same toward me. I think she could read John's intentions and knew they were innocent and platonic. I think she could also read mine.

So my dating life with Penny was tricky. John often dropped me off a few blocks from Penny's, picked her up, and then retrieved me. We were discovered once, when Penny's father was driving home and spotted me lurking along the roadway. Not much came of it; we were in love and resolute.

After graduation, John went on to college at Notre Dame, and we saw less of each other. But there were still adventures to be had. One weekend, when he was home from college, we had another memorable one.

It began at his house in Richfield, where we got into his brand new 1965 Oldsmobile Cutlass and headed for Ellsworth. John had a date with his own Judy, and I was going "out drinking" with Billy.

We split up. I arrived home in Ellsworth very late, and John's Cutlass wasn't in the driveway. Despite appearances, he was indeed home and had been watching for me. When I pulled into the driveway, he came walking out of the house—with his arm in a sling.

"Scratch one 1965 Cutlass," he said.

After taking Judy to a movie in Red Wing and returning her home, he'd fallen asleep at the wheel, then veered off the highway and into a telephone pole, demolishing his wonderful car.

Before shedding too many tears for John, remember: He had a very understanding father who was always willing to advance him money. It was not long before we were back riding around in another new car—this time a *Corvette!* It was a beautiful blue convertible with a 350 horsepower, 327 cubic-inch engine. It also had a four-on-the-floor transmission and a speedometer that went up to 160 miles per hour. I'm not sure we ever got it there, but with that giant motor and small fiber-glass body, the car could absolutely fly!

12

Marriage and Family

In those days, single young people were almost always coupled up. After I moved to prep school at St. John's and left Judy behind, I was due to re-couple, and the pool of lovely candidates of classy, rich gals looked inexhaustible. True to form, my old buddy and former girlfriend-finder, Rich, had been burrowing away at Holy Angels. He'd again found the "girl of his dreams." Her name was Rosemary.

Rich was known as "Bump" in those days, as the campus barber had once commented that the little protrusion at the lower base of his skull was rather pronounced. Well, that's all it took to let loose the fierce and ever-ready teasing boarding school boys fed on. And the name totally stuck. I should mention I was called "Hinse" (later formalized to "Hinsel"), owing to a letter I received from my dear small-town girlfriend Judy, where she had misspelled my name.

Anyway, it seemed Bump and I had a common bond, and it wasn't sports or academics. We were both consumed with thinking about girls! I think we also had a shared vision of the perfect woman. Our definition, in order of priority: cute, smart, shapely, preferably blonde, and a touch profane. With that target, an expensive private girls' school was exactly the right hunting ground. Bump had been successful with Rosemary, but history was circling. I don't know if it was a case of me always stealing his perfect prizes, or if he was always just moving on. Nonetheless, I know that I once again felt wonderfully matched with his new choice.

So began a couple years of Rosemary and I dating and becoming emotionally attached. She lived at home initially, but by then I had an apartment in Prescott, which was a nice spot to hang out, leading eventually to co-habitation. This was followed by a *Friends* stint, where she joined John, Billy, and I in an old two-story house we rented on the Mississippi. It had been condemned by the City of Prescott, but they were willing to rent it to us (possibly due to my relationship with the McGrath family). After all, they owned both the bank (my dad's bank, with branches in both towns) and the hospital where I worked. The rent was $25 a month, or $8.33 per person. It did have running water, but no furniture—just mattresses on the living room floor. I don't recall if we had electricity, but there was definitely no heat. When fall rolled around, we needed new arrangements. It was time for the new school year, and John simply returned to Notre Dame while Rosemary and I moved into a one-room apartment above the laundromat on Prescott's main drag. These were happy days for us, and we both had halfway decent cars. Rose had a cute little Buick Special, and I had my trusty Pontiac from Jeanine. I had a full-time job at the hospital, and I was attending college at River Falls.

As Rosemary and I continued to date and spend more time together in our Prescott apartment, we decided it was time for marriage. We informed and gained the consent of the necessary folks, and the event was planned. It was not to be a modest affair, but the full-blown, all-the-relatives *masterpiece* of which she'd always dreamed. John was, of course, my best man. Billy stood right next him, along with some pal of Rosemary's.

When the ordeal finally wound down, we piled everything into our old Chevy station wagon and headed for Florida (for some reason, I was *always* headed to the coast). From there, it was a solid drive, straight southeast until we reached the Atlantic Ocean. We were both awed at our first sight of an ocean and walked down to touch the water at Cocoa Beach. Feeling enchanted, we decided to stay right there. We found temporary living in a cheap motel, and I went out to look for a job.

Having never had a real job and never looked for one, I was naive and didn't know where to begin. I got a lead for a national lending chain called General Electric Credit, an arm of GE that pushed sales by financing new TVs and appliances. The interview went well. Because of my impressive credentials (I had a car and spoke English) I was hired immediately. I became a suit-wearing, leg-busting, bill collector!

My territory ran from Titusville to Vera Beach—a ninety-mile stretch of mostly run-down resort communities. My assignments took me into the poorest communities of color, where many residents were the proud owners of big, console-style color TVs. I lacked the understanding then of what a great equalizer a large TV was between the rich and the poor. Unfortunately, many of these owners were not paying for their possessions in a timely manner. The TVs (and the occasional second appliance) needed to be repossessed, and I was knocking on doors to do so. At the time, I looked about fourteen. I stood roughly five feet and ten inches and weighed about 140 pounds. My short blond hair nicely complemented my super-white skin. Our trusty Chevy wagon was the perfect repo car.

I lasted less than six months, and even that was a grueling challenge. But I had a wife to support, and we were well on our way to having a baby, so I had no choice. We lived in a non-air-conditioned mobile home then, and Rosemary—never a tall person—was of about equal height and width. Her stature, plus being three weeks overdue in the heat of southern Florida, did not make her a happy wife. So it was with a relief when, late one September afternoon, we headed off to the nearest hospital in Melbourne. A few hours later, Tara was born.

13

Another Love of My Life

Baby Tara was a total joy from the first moment of her life. Now it was the three of us—bound together in a happy little family, with the minor discomfort of Dad hating his job, which wasn't going to last much longer. I spent my days in the office and nights out on my treacherous repossession rounds. I asked the people I met for their past-due balances, but they never paid. Most of the time, I left with their TV, unplugging it from whatever the family and kids were watching.

One night, when Tara was about three weeks old, I came home utterly stressed out and announced that I had quit my job and we were going to move back to Minnesota. There was no argument from Rose. She understood. She knew the job was a real disaster for me—what she did not know was that I had just been fired. And we were both homesick. We'd had only one visitor our whole time there, when John had driven down from Minneapolis. It was a thirty-hour trip nonstop in his big, yellow 1960 Oldsmobile convertible. He arrived tired and sunburned, but we were thrilled to see him and had a great time together. We lived in an upstairs apartment then, right on the beach, and John and I spent hours bodysurfing—quite a treat for a couple of guys from the land-locked Midwest. Yet Rosemary and I were equally pleased when he finally decided to leave, as we'd become eager to have our twosome life back.

John's visit had been our only contact with our family and friends, and we grew steadily more homesick. The grandparents needed to see the baby, I was out of a job, and there wasn't anything holding us in Florida—certainly not the cockroaches, with the sickening *shshshshsh* sound they made whenever you turned on the lights, sending them all slithering into hiding. We were ready to hit the road north. We made a little bed for three-week-old Tara in the back of the station wagon and drove the entire way nonstop.

In Minnesota, we initially moved in with Rosemary's mom, who had a small "garden-level" apartment in Minneapolis. Her mom was always supportive and welcoming, but now that we were and married and used to having our own place, we were ready to move on, and I needed to get going on my job search. I figured that now, with a vast career in finance under my belt, I'd be a shoo-in at another collection agency.

Sure enough, I found my way to the Community Credit Company. They had offices all around the Twin Cities and could always use another collector. I was assigned to their office in White Bear Lake, and we quickly moved into the first affordable place we could find, which was an older rental duplex in South St. Paul. This was not a home we enjoyed. It was cheap, dark, and small, and we had picked up a little dog that covered the entire basement floor with dog poop. Our unhappiness there, however, may have been a foreshadowing of more serious trouble ahead.

We soon found ourselves a terrific little apartment on the north side of St. Paul. I loved this apartment. It was much closer to work, and it was bright and sunny, on the third floor and with a large balcony overlooking the I-35 freeway. I would sit there for hours in the blissful company of my baby girl, just watching the traffic. Our apartment was near enough to Rosemary's mom's place, so it wasn't bad for dropping Tara off with grandma when we both needed to be someplace. I went to work every day, and Rosemary renewed friendships in Minneapolis that she had suddenly abandoned in her rush to move to Florida. So I was satisfied with my desk job, and with Rosemary gone a lot, I had tons of time to be home with Tara. It was a mostly happy time … until one day, it all came thunderously crashing down.

Courtesy of Wikimedia Commons (Charles Levy).

14

The Day the World Ended

After coming home from a routine day at work, I found both Rosemary and Tara had gone and there was a note on the kitchen table. It said that we were going to get a separation, and that Tara would stay with Rose. I lost it. For the first time in my young life, I was slapped in the face with a reality that felt unbearable. I actually dropped to the floor, crying. I went into the street and out onto the freeway and walked, weeping madly in the 5:00 p.m. traffic. Eventually, Rosemary found me and took me home.

The pain was enormous. This was over fifty years ago, and the memory is still deeply uncomfortable. I'd led a pretty lucky, somewhat sheltered life, and this was my first dose of some tough, adult reality.

I located a bedroom in a boarding house with a handful of much-older, single men. There was a shared bath, and we had one prepared, communal meal each evening. Again, I found myself in a place I didn't belong. It reminded me of the Gregory

Corso poem "Marriage," where he despairs at the solitude of living alone.

The year was 1968. The Vietnam War was raging, Martin Luther King was assassinated, Bobby Kennedy was assassinated, there were riots at the Democratic National Convention, and Nixon was elected. I felt that the world was simply coming apart. My personal life was in complete shambles.

The awkward life of me in the old men's home and Tara mostly with her mom lasted about a year. The next summer, I went to National Guard summer camp for two weeks, feeling unsettled and depressed. But the two weeks of marching and working out in the hot sun with other weekend warriors proved to be just the jolt I needed, and I ended up having one of those rare epiphanies.

I was sitting alone on the steps outside the barracks at sunset when I said to myself: *This is bullshit! As soon as I get home, I'm marching over to my Rosemary and Tara's house and demanding a resolution.*

I was prepared for the worst, but I wanted and expected the best: time to reunite! An apt description of me would've been that I was "full of myself."

It was a hot July day when I returned from camp and drove straight to the apartment, ready for a confrontation. I took a deep breath and knocked on the door. I jolted back when the door opened.

Whoa! Who is this? I thought. Little did I know that the next few moments would seal my fate forever.

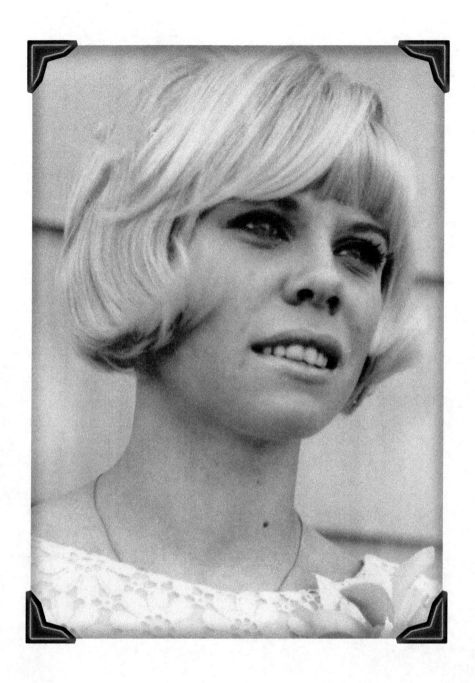

15

Love at First Sight

Every time I think of this scene—Jean standing in the doorway, with her long blonde hair and short dress, her body silhouetted in the setting sun—my heart skips a beat. It really was love at first sight. I was hooked.

Yes, she was there babysitting Tara. When I explained that I was Tara's father, she invited me in, and we sat on the floor and talked—through the night and into the morning hours. Though the clock moved toward dawn, my life stood still. The long search for the perfect woman had just ended in a spectacular, permanent finale! The quest itself had been long and arduous, but the result proved it all worthwhile … in fact, it was magnificent. In my mind, a big curtain came down amid riotous applause.

16

The Summer of 1969

Fresh summer love with a touch of adultery was an intoxicating mix. We were, after all, both married, though neither of us felt much like it. Jean's husband was on an archaeological dig in Guatemala as part of his graduate work at the university. The school would've paid for her to be with him, but there was increasing marital disharmony that told her to stay back. My wife, Rose, was searching out her life in new directions, giving me a lot of time to be with Tara. At the time, both marriages were on trial separations, having somehow gone awry. In hindsight, we had such amazing luck.

One evening, we walked to a nearby park for a Credence Clearwater Revival concert, a band we both liked. We stood there, feeling entranced in the moment. The music was great, but I think we could've gone to a dogfight and had about the same rapt experience.

To top off the summer dream, Jean drove a small sports car—a Triumph Spitfire. That was one more thing this small-town kid had never experienced. The car had tan leather seats, a four-speed transmission, and an open top that allowed Jean's long blonde hair to sail in the summer wind. I joked that I wasn't sure if I loved her or her car more. It was close. So many years later, I still have both.

By great fortune, John also found a genuine girlfriend that summer. He'd made new friends at his job at the Richfield Liquor Store. These friends had a party one night, where he met this tall and very attractive brunette. Lynne was great fun, and she truly liked John. It was a breakthrough of sorts as, although John had been on plenty of dates, this was his first serious romantic connection. They were a wonderful fit. By late summer, they were looking more and more like a permanent deal. In December, he bought her a diamond. The summer of 1969 was going to go into the history books with another big milestone for both of us.

Heartbreakingly, John had the ring back a few months later. The summer ended badly for me as well. Jean's husband returned from Guatemala with the intent of resuming his marriage. He and I had both become cast-offs. I had already experienced marital breakup, and I was on the road to recovery. Unfortunately for him, I'd been driving down this recovery road in *his car* and with *his wife*. He still had the trauma of breakup ahead of him—or so I dearly hoped.

One afternoon in early fall, I bade farewell to Jean with enormous despair as she moved to Boston. Her husband was enrolled in the doctoral program at Harvard, and Jean had found a job in the Harvard mail department. Shortly after the move, Jean realized that staying with her husband wasn't in the cards because of his physical and mental abuse. She found an apartment and moved out.

Jean's job at Harvard was a godsend, as she was soon in the Harvard Infirmary with her first major lupus flare-up since her diagnosis years earlier. Until then, she had suffered quietly with the disease, always keeping aspirin in her system, and the lupus had stayed mostly in remission. The Harvard Infirmary was a high-class facility, and it was only her marriage to a student that entitled her to be there. After a few weeks, she was moved to intensive care at Massachusetts General Hospital, where her symptoms were brought under control. After lots of her new best friend—corticosteroids (prednisone)—and nearly three months of having her wacky immune system suppressed, she returned to her single apartment.

17

Hitchhiking to Boston

With Jean living alone, I was able to call her freely, and one call brought a life-changing question. I was at work at the First National Bank of Minneapolis. I'd unceremoniously moved on from Community Credit. All I remember is that she asked me, "Aren't you going to come out here?"

Honestly, I about fell over. Somehow, I did not understand she still held these feelings for me. I hung up the phone and told my boss I was quitting to move east. I packed up, gave away my meager belongings, took my knapsack, walked down to the freeway ramp, and stuck out my thumb, looking for a ride to Boston.

I had phenomenally good luck hitchhiking. It was summer, and I could sleep in ditches, just a bit off the highway. I made it to Boston in a just few days and somehow found my way to a subway station. From there, it was a route straight up the Red Line to Cambridge. I was closing in.

I arrived in Cambridge at Harvard Square and walked the few blocks to Jean's apartment. I think I called her from the subway station, but as I stood in front of the building, something told me to stop and reflect for a moment. *This step may be for the rest of your life.* I sat down on the curb across the street and did a full stop-and-think. Then I crossed the street to her apartment; once more, I was knocking on a door and waiting—only this time I *knew* it would be Jean coming to the door.

Jean had her own her bedroom, but she shared the kitchen, living room, and bath with three others, a gal and two guys. This was the sixties—the free-loving, war-protesting, loud-rocking, dope-smoking era. Cambridge, Massachusetts, was as much at the center of it all as any place. It was quite a change for a little gal from Moorhead … and for me, for that matter.

When I first saw her, there was one obvious change: She had big puffy cheeks crowding her wire-rim glasses, a common prednisone side effect. She had developed this look gradually and was now accustomed to it, but it was new to me and more than a little shocking. It was another brief stop-and-reflect moment, but once we started talking it was all Jean. I was still nuts about her.

18

Life in the Big City

I became the fifth resident of Jean's apartment. It was an acceptable but far from an ideal arrangement, and we soon found ourselves a new apartment.

Of course, I needed a job. With my vast experience in the banking industry, I called up the big bank across the street from where Jean worked and asked about employment prospects. One call, one interview, and Jean and I were walking to and from work together. Picture us all dressed up for work: Jean, a Harvard University employee, and me, a full-time, suit-and-tie *banker* with the Harvard Trust Company. I'll bet my dad loved hearing that!

It was here that our life together really began. We went to movies, discovered restaurants that we still remember, and smoked a little dope out on our lovely balcony (which was actually just a landing for the fire escape). This "balcony" was in a dark, gloomy alley, accessible through the one window of our one-room apartment. Its view was the other side of our

U-shaped building. But if you leaned out far enough and looked to your left, you could see the Boston skyline in the distance. It was our perfect getaway.

This was also where my dear little Lutheran wife, of such good upbringing, introduced me to drugs—marijuana, hash, and mescaline (a hallucinogenic much like acid or LSD). We only did the acid-tripping mescaline a few times (and never out on the fire escape!) but I am forever grateful for having had these experiences. An extended hallucinogenic episode is not something that can be easily described. Although they are still on the street, these drugs are now also used in a variety of medical treatments, including for mental illness. For me, having these experiences was educational and worthwhile. And we were always very cautious when we were tripping, with the exception of the one time we decided to go to the grocery store. Big mistake.

Before the story of two-hippies-turning-into-hopeless-drug-addicts develops any more steam, let me say that this was a very minor part of our life. We were, in fact, a quite stable and employed young Midwestern couple. Jean's brother, Ted, lived in a Boston suburb with his wife, Sandy, and their two little daughters. My daughter-starved soul fell for them hopelessly. Ted was a resident-in-training at Tufts University School of Medicine. He deeply cared for and always looked after his sickly little sister, so for quite a while he wasn't informed of her new living arrangement.

Knowing he was coming to check on Jean one evening, I went up onto the roof of the apartment building to wait out his visit. Ever since the Coca-Cola Bottling Company in East Ellsworth, I was destined for rooftops—although this one was up ten stories. Peering over the top of the front ledge, I got my first look at Ted as I watched him arrive and leave. It didn't take very long for us to come clean with Ted and Sandy, and we began a long and enduring friendship that included, with great pleasure, babysitting. I remained deeply, though somewhat unconsciously, heartsick over Tara. Their daughters, Kristin and Brittany, brought this into focus. Jean could readily see it, but she had also been more aware than me of the heartbreak and depression that lurked not far beneath my carefree surface.

Ted may also have noticed. Beyond being in medical school, Ted was one very smart guy, keenly observant, witty, and charming. But he could also become deadly serious. I have seen him walk into a hospital ER, calm everyone down, and take full command. It is fair to say I admired him immensely. But he was in med school full time, worked days in the hospital and the ER on weekends, and studied every night. In the evenings, when he had time to be with us, he would continually doze off, often in the middle of the conversation … sometimes when he was the one talking. But again, I admired him greatly.

We were at an experimenting time in our life and that applied to a lot of areas. Despite our happiness together, with comfortable living and good jobs, Jean and I were restless. The

Wild West called. Ultimately, we answered the call, bought a car, and headed for Eugene, Oregon. Why Eugene? No idea. Another coast to explore? Still today, neither of us has ever been there. But away we went. We had our little four-hundred-dollar Fiat, about two hundred dollars in cash, and my old Army tent. It all seemed perfectly reasonable to us.

The only surviving picture of Jean and me in those years shows us standing together in my parents' driveway in Ellsworth (about halfway between Boston and Eugene). Jean's shy caution and my recklessness are both on full display. At the time, my folks were big fans of my wife, Rosemary, and especially of Tara. They despaired at our breakup and always held hopes of us reuniting. They were also kept in the dark for a long time about our separation. Those hopes continued to recede, and Jean's natural good impression helped immensely. Here was a cute, wholesome, small-town gal—despite the fact she was married and traveling the country with an already-married man. But that man was their very own irresponsible, but always-forgiven, little boy.

19

Family Tragedy

Our visit with my parents was met with a sudden and tragic interruption. We received a call at my parents' house from Jean's mom, but she didn't ask for Jean. She wanted to talk to me.

Jean's beloved dad had just died, and she asked me to tell her. He was young, only fifty-three years old—a healthy working man who had dropped dead of a heart attack at home. An ambulance had been called, but it was too late. He had been feeling some warning signs and, ironically, had a visit to a cardiologist scheduled for the next day.

I faced the task of telling Jean—and it was horrible. This was an especially close family, and her dad was the centerpiece. She was devastated. The next day, she flew to Fargo–Moorhead for the funeral. I followed in our car a few days later, still quite an outsider to her family. But I had met her mom, Borgie, who would become one of the most important and loved people in my life.

We'd actually traveled to Moorhead once before, during our romantic first summer. Her family only knew that poor little Jeanie was living alone down in the Big City while her husband was in Guatemala. We drove her Triumph for the four-hour trip. Once again, along came the trusty old Army tent. Jean dropped me off at a nearby sewer plant—a collection of buildings and smelly holding tanks in the woods, well-suited for hiding a little tent and only a few blocks from the family home. It was also close enough for a nightly visit.

At the time, Jean lived alone in her apartment near the University of Minnesota, where she had a job in the admissions department. She made friends with the young colleague working alongside her. This gal was having marital issues too, so they commiserated. I remember Rosemary coming home and talking about her new friend at work. In fact, I once picked up Rosemary from work, and she asked that we give her friend a ride home, so we did. Never really met her … just some blonde sat in the back seat.

This trip for Jean's father's funeral was entirely different. Our relationship had been outed somewhere along the line, probably part of our friendship with Ted and his family. I'd also been tacitly accepted without much scrutiny. Jean's husband had been an "adopted" part of their family for years. His mother had left home, abandoning him to a disjointed and abusive life with his father. Even though—or perhaps because— he was so well-known to Jean's family, no one was very happy about her marrying him. Early in their marriage, he became abusive at home, like his father, and Jean realized her bad decision. His trip to Guatemala had been a godsend for her. Of course, it was certainly a godsend for me!

Since our relationship was now in the open, the family gatherings that followed the funeral served as my introduction to the Eastlunds (Jean's maiden name, which also appears as the dedication for my later doctoral dissertation). I was enthralled with her Jean's family. She had three brothers—two older, Ted and Larry, and one younger, Jonnie. The family owned a cabin on a nearby lake. As soon as her mom ("Borgie" to all, including her kids) was up for it, we traveled there and hung out in the aftermath of their loss.

Borgie was in miserable shape emotionally and relied on Valium to get her through the day. She was, however, a person of remarkable inner strength, energy, and vitality—much of which had been stifled in her very traditional role as a fifties mom and housewife. Jean's mild-mannered dad, Phil, was the slyly humorous and entertaining one. But in an ironic twist of fate, the person Borgie was inside rose into full bloom as her life moved forward without him—an actualization of a Borgie who may never have existed under other circumstances.

I recently had the honor of giving the eulogy at her funeral and was deeply saddened (and still am) to recount the incredible person she was. I had come to love her. I also knew it was a requited love, as if she had another son. Her younger two sons, Ted and Jonnie, were to become like brothers to me; her eldest, Larry, was to die at the same age as his father had passed and from the same cause. Ted also had a heart attack when he reached about that age, but he managed to get to a hospital in time for an emergency bypass. Jean was lucky to be a girl.

20

Back in the World of Psychiatric Care

It was soon time for the Gary and Jean show to get back on the road. We packed up our little car, windows covered with reddish tint to protect our lupus patient from the sun, and resumed the trek to Eugene. That car was unbelievable. We bought it for four hundred dollars in Boston, and it took us everywhere in the country for years; we finally sold it some twenty years later, still running.

Traveling west, we slept in the old Army tent. We never looked for campgrounds, but we found out-of-the-way spots. Crossing the Rocky Mountains, we woke up to snow on the tent one morning, but we shared a sleeping bag (also Army-issue), so we were never cold … or very far apart. Our day-to-day destination seemed to shift around, even though Eugene was always on the far horizon.

Traveling without any purpose or destination can lead you to unexpected places. We somehow found ourselves in the southwestern states and made a spontaneous decision to go to L.A. and visit my now-married, long-ago girlfriend, Penny. All I can say is that it seemed to make sense then. I hadn't had any contact with her for years, so how we knew all this stuff about each other back then, before any email or cell phones, is a bit mysterious.

We arrived in Los Angeles one afternoon and checked in at a Motel 6. This arrangement appealed to our frugality, as the name originally stood for the fact that the rooms were six dollars per night. I remember being disappointed that they had gone up to eight dollars, as we had very little money. The two hundred dollars we left Boston with wasn't going to last forever (and yes, this was before credit cards). Plus, we'd been on the road a couple of weeks.

From the motel, we called Penny and her husband and were enthusiastically invited over. In the style of the day, we sat on the floor and listened to music (they introduced us to punk music, Patti Smith in particular). We smoked a little grass and then slept over for whatever was left of the night. I know it was a Saturday night, because in the morning I was looking through the Sunday paper and came across a want ad describing a job *for a couple*. "Resident managers for a psychiatric board and care facility" … whatever that was.

At the time, California was closing and emptying its ill-reputed state mental institutions, giving rise to a sorely unregulated industry for housing mentally ill patients. All it took was an apartment building or motel that could be converted to offer single-occupancy rooms (or sometimes double-occupancy), plus a central dining room with a kitchen and cook. You could house any number of residents and bill the State of California for the monthly room and board.

Vernmark Manor was one such facility, and on Monday morning we called them up, resulting in an interview appointment that day. Remembering the "married couple" stipulation in the ad, we stopped at a pawn shop on Santa Monica Boulevard and bought two gold wedding rings (nine dollars total). We now qualified for the job. We would also soon learn that "resident manager" did not refer to managing the residents; it meant *being* the managers *and living in the residence.* We moved into our new home that night.

Vernmark Manor was not in a good neighborhood, to say the least. It was in South L.A., just south of the freeway (I-10) and on the northern edge of Watts. Vernmark had over 120 residents, all recently released, psychiatrically disabled adults; there was a mix of sexes, races, diagnoses, and severity, as well as a wide range of behavioral problems. The owner and executive director (*not* in residence) was a tall and very intimidating Black man with a personality straight out of a Quentin Tarantino movie. He was an imposing presence and had a big corner office with a huge desk—all wood-paneled, dark, and rich. It was entirely out of character with the rest of the shabby facility.

The job was basically to move into the resident managers' apartment and *do everything.* The only other staff were a cook and a janitor, neither of whom lived there. Doing everything included trying to keep order, guiding lost souls back to their rooms (repeatedly), and distributing medications. Almost all the residents took heavy doses of psychotropics, such as Haldol and Thorazine. Jean was in charge of medications (with no related training or education whatsoever). The medicines were housed in a large walk-in closet of sorts, along with the prescriptions and patient charts. Morning, noon, and night, the residents would line up in the hallway and, one-by-one, present themselves to Jean's little half-door for their meds. She would dispense their doses (and watch that they consumed them). She also supplied me with meds to distribute to patients who needed to have them brought to their rooms—or brought wherever I could find them. Keep in mind, these were people who would have been held in padded cells at the state mental hospital, and these medications were, in theory, their ticket to live in the community. Still, these could be dangerous people. We learned later that the last person doing Jean's job had been stabbed.

I worked mostly on activities. That covered quite the variety, from breaking up fights to removing contraband (like alcohol) from resident rooms and taking day trips in the facility's eleven-passenger van. The sprawling city of L.A. was perfect, as it had an abundance of interesting sites, from Sunset Strip to the Santa Monica Pier. You could go from a sunny ocean beach to a snowy mountaintop on the same day. We lasted in this crazy job for over a year.

In 1971, in what was the dead of winter back home, we were treated to two equally dramatic family visits. The first was from Jean's mom and little brother Jonnie, now seventeen. It gave them a retreat from the lonely, post-Dad home they shared. They were heading for a winter vacation in Hawaii. The drama of this particular event was all in our preparation, as they planned on spending the night with us, and Jean felt her mom would be more comfortable visiting and sleeping *under the same roof* if we were married. So we put together a rather unromantic plan: We needed a marriage license and a venue, along with a legal officiant. We were able to secure both for the same day.

We had to take a trip to the city courthouse in old downtown L.A. (where few tourists ever ventured) for the license; then, somehow, we found a curious little enterprise in Watts that would marry us that day. It was difficult as heck to get a day off from our job, so we scheduled a 4:00 p.m. wedding with a quick stop downtown to pick up our license. Unfortunately, while we were in the courthouse getting our marriage license, our car was towed. I had parked in a no-parking spot, as we were in a hurry and I thought it would be a quick in-and-out. I was reminded of my poor judgment by my soon-to-be bride, but it didn't derail our plans. Although someone a little less love-struck might have observed a tiny hint of untold similar rebukes in my future.

We made it to the wedding chapel on time, and it was something to behold. Located in the dead center of Watts, it was a tiny, pink, one-room building with dimensions somewhere between a garage and a dollhouse. We were met by a quiet, elderly Black Baptist minister who was to officiate and sanctify this union. The place had barely room for the two of us, plus the pastor and two elderly ladies who served as the required witnesses. To make the event even more spectacular, Jean was offered a small vase of dusty plastic flowers to hold for an additional fifteen dollars. I believe we declined. The ceremony was short, but as quite a happy surprise, the pastor gave us a marvelous, thoughtful little talk, highlighting the importance of this moment and the commitment we were making to each other. He was serious, genuine, and not at all rehearsed. He did a great job and it stuck. I wish we could thank him. Our glamorous honeymoon was one night at the nearby Holiday Inn, a step up from the old Motel 6.

We returned to Vernmark Manor the next day and remained carefree and happy in our perilous little world. In my activities manager role, I opened a small snack shop and convenience store. Yes, this was my third Corner Bar and Counseling Center, though I'd not yet coined the term. It followed on the heels of the lemonade stand and the root beer stand—one more place to serve my unshakable social drive.

Our second dramatic visit was from my parents, as always checking on their ever-wayward son. The drama of this visit was created by whom they had arranged to bring with them— my four-year-old Tara! My heart burst with both joy and sorrow as I held the toddler. The five of us went on a trip to

Disneyland, and I especially remember she and I riding through the "It's a Small World" together. For a few precious minutes, it was.

But Tara had a new stepdad now, and at her formative age that was distressing for me. When they asked if I would release my parental rights so the new dad could officially adopt Tara, I consented, feeling that in the end it would be best for her. Despite all the complicated dynamics, I always felt I'd deserted her.

The
Kangaroo
Camper

21

The Kangaroo Camper

While living in L.A., Jean and I bought our Kangaroo Camper. Designed to attach to the top and rear of a Volkswagen Beetle, it worked perfectly on our Fiat sedan. When closed, it was about a foot above the roof of the car; it was larger toward the back, and when opened, it revealed a fold-down ladder and a little entry area with a sink. When the camper was open, the roof sloped down toward the front, with canvas sides and a full-size foam bed. We loved this thing. I'll always remember our first outing, when we camped on Santa Barbara Beach—a night in our fun new rig, relaxing with the sounds of the ocean. The Kangaroo was part of our life for a very long time, even residing for a time in our driveway in Hudson, Wisconsin.

Our life in L.A. and our stint at Vernmark Manor ended, much as it had begun, with yet *another* dose of drama. We were awakened by a call in the middle of the night from a caller who claimed to have been observing us (he had some details, like a description of our car). He warned us we were going to encounter some dangerous trouble if we did not get out of town … now!

We speculated the call must have been inspired by one of our residents, as we had plenty of worrisome ones and some from whose rooms I'd recently been removing a lot of contraband, especially alcohol. But who this caller was really didn't matter— he sounded awfully serious, and we believed him. We followed his instructions and prepared to leave by the end of the week. As always, we had very little money, but the Kangaroo Camper was a lifesaver. We were soon back on the road, destination uncertain.

22

Getting Serious About Life

We spent our first night parked in the open desert northeast of L.A. The Kangaroo was ideal, as we would not have enjoyed a night on the desert floor. The next afternoon, we came across a gravel side road leading down to what looked like an alluring little valley. We were anticipating a pleasant night under the trees, until we had to stop for a spider in the middle of the road. Yes, we had to stop the car. This was the largest tarantula we had ever seen. I got out and took a quick look at this soft-ball-sized creature blocking our way, then we got the heck out of there.

Little things were adding up to attract us to the comforts of being back home. With lots of time to talk, we decided it made the most sense to head to Jean's old home in Moorhead. Her mom was there with just Jonnie now. Her old room was empty, and her mom would surely welcome us. We knew it would be wonderful for her; little did we know what a benefit it would be for Jon, who was not yet old enough to buy beer (and I was). And that was the starting point of my great, life-long brotherly bond with Jon.

Moorhead also presented us the opportunity to return to school, and we both enrolled at Moorhead State College. Jean continued in undergraduate psychology. I completed my bachelor's in psychology and master's in counseling. Jean found a new appreciation of education, and I found myself enjoying school for the first time. Some measure of maturity had been acquired during our wandering years, and I was suddenly ready to learn. An Art 101 class made a huge impression on me. I may not have quite turned the corner, but there was hope.

We soon found another job where we could work together—this time as resident managers of a small group home. It was an older house with ten adult men, each with severe intellectual disabilities—what was then called "mental retardation." As anyone familiar with the traits that typify this population will attest, they were wonderful, interesting, and above all the most loving individuals. Most were in shared bedrooms; three were brothers, and two of these were twins. Jean and I had a large bedroom with our own bathroom on the main floor. Everything else was communal.

Jean made the meals, served around one large table. It's a memory that's hard to picture—Jean making and serving three meals a day for twelve people—but she did it. She also cleaned, did the laundry, kept the medical files, and did just about everything else needed to care for a large group of people.

The truth is, Jean had some fabulous help: Frank, the shyest brother, made the coffee every morning and called out to his brother when it was ready.

"Coffee time, Emil!" (A phrase used in our house to this day.)

If there were any loud noises in the kitchen, you could count on Albert, the third brother, to shout, "Knock a house down!" I had duties too, but mostly I was in school. This group-home saga added a new chapter that was provocative and deeply educational for us.

As I neared the end of my graduate degree, I was relieved that I was finally done with school. Then another of those milestone events occurred. I was in a casual meeting with my advisor, Dr. Dean Olson, when out of the blue he said that I was going to go on and get my doctoral degree! Without waiting for my response, he turned in his chair, picked up the phone, and called the dean of the Graduate School of Counseling at the University of South Dakota in Vermillion. He announced he was sending down a new student for the doctoral program. I went home and told a very surprised wife that we were moving to Vermillion.

23

The Couple Moving in at 24 Walnut Street

Compared to the metropolis of Fargo–Moorhead, Vermillion was a small town. We called to have our water turned on, and I was about to tell the utility guy the address, when he said, "Yeah, I saw you drive into town. Aren't you the couple moving into 24 Walnut Street?"

Because it housed the main campus of the university, Vermillion seemed larger than it actually was; take away the school and students and the town hardly existed. On the other hand, it was the quintessential college town. Everything revolved around the students. Bars, restaurants, shops, and activities all served the students. It was a great place to live.

Jean and I both attended school full time and had no employment. Jean finished her psychology degree and entered the master's program in school psychology, and I entered the doctoral program in counseling psychology. The dozen other doctoral students provided a ready-made social group. And we were soon to add another fantastic element.

In Moorhead, we'd made friends with another couple, Frank and Linda. Frank was my supervisor at the Southeast Mental Health Center, where I completed my internship for the master's program. The four of us developed a special bond. They'd lived just across the river, in the twin town of Fargo. Despite the fact that they had two small children, had just purchased their house, were settled in, and were relieved to be done with school ... we couldn't resist inviting them to Vermillion. One night, we simply called them up and made our pitch. Lo and behold, they accepted our invitation! For Frank, the idea of becoming Dr. Buzzetta was just too tempting. From there, we embarked on a marvelous, carefree student life—living on school loans and, in our case, financial help from my always-supportive parents. We must have realized this might be our last great carefree chapter, because we sure made the most of it.

Aside from completing our required doctoral dissertations, neither Frank nor I spent much time studying. The school's student center had a fabulous pool and billiards room, and we had discovered the addictive game of bottle pool, where you play standard billiards while avoid upsetting an upside-down leather bottle that sits precariously in the middle of the table. We had that special competitiveness that creeps up among very close friends, and the hours passed too easily. Our wives would quickly confirm this.

With Frank and Linda—as well as with our friends Bob and Bev, and sometimes all six of us—we slipped easily into craziness. Me more than the others, of course. On some of these occasions, we made memories that stick with us.

For example, we loved playing cards with Frank and Linda. One night, when I left the table to go to their bathroom, I came back wearing only Linda's yellow bikini, which she had left temptingly hanging there to dry. On another night, based on someone's dare, I climbed to the top of the city water tower. What made the incident all the goofier is that I did it stark naked. I don't think it takes a psychologist to see a theme here.

Several years ago—I remember exactly where I was and what I was doing—I got a call from Linda. Frank had just died. Just out of the blue, with no warning, he simply died. He went out to get the mail, and Linda saw him fall down at the mailbox. The doctors later said he was dead before he hit the ground. She and their three children were in shock and disbelief. I broke down crying for only the second time I can remember in my adult life. Frank was gone, and Linda's life was forever changed. She tried to start over, but she was emotionally crumbled and passed away a few years later.

As with most colleges, USD had a placement office that provided resources to help graduating students find their next move. One day, as I neared the end of my studies, I was looking through materials in this office and came across an ad for a job as director of county social services in Hudson, Wisconsin. It required a master's degree, and the newly minted Dr. Gary Hines should be a natural.

It's funny how in hindsight things look so auspicious. We drove to Hudson and stayed with my parents in nearby Ellsworth. As expected, the job interview went great. It was a regular love-in visit with everyone in the office. We also loved Hudson. It was a June day, and everything was blooming and green and beautiful. It looked and smelled like heaven—flowers everywhere, tree-lined streets, and colossal old homes.

We were so impressed we decided to look at possible places to live. Why put it off?

24

Finding Home

I realize now what a slam dunk our search in Hudson was. Jean had never (and still *has* never) met a house she didn't love. The house we found might have needed a wall bumped out here or there—one of her favorite pursuits—but finding one to buy was an absolute sure thing, and we did it.

It was an older home on the edge of the downtown, and the upstairs windows had views of the St. Croix River. We left them an offer just under their asking price of $22,000. Later that day, back in Vermillion, we sealed the deal over the phone. We were overjoyed. Everything was falling into place, and we felt like we were living on a cloud.

The cloud, unfortunately, was fleeting. Before nightfall, another phone call brought the shocking news that I did not get the job. We later learned it had been set for an internal candidate all along, but the county had been required to go through the motions of interviewing applicants. So we now owned a house in Hudson, but I did not have the job we were moving there for.

I phoned my old friend, John, and shared my predicament. He reminded me that his cousin, Nancy, was a counselor at a rehabilitation center in the Twin Cities. It might be worth contacting her. I knew Nancy a little and was happy to give her a call, even though I felt it was a bit of a long shot. It couldn't hurt.

Nancy did know of a possible opening. The organization she worked for had just received a federal grant, and the director was hiring staff. The agency was the Minneapolis Rehabilitation Center (MRC). Using Nancy as a reference turned out to be important, as she was a stable, respected member of the MRC staff. The director, Nelson Otto, was quite a character, but we hit it off. I was soon the program coordinator for the Center for Continuing Education (CCE). My salary was $12,000 a year—not great, but enough to live on and cover house payments.

This federal grant was to provide continuing education for rehab counselors. It proposed a series of two- or three-day workshops on different elements of counseling. It wasn't defined much further than that. By lucky coincidence, I had relevant experience. At that time, all doctoral programs required completion of a dissertation, a major peer-reviewed and published study. It was a hurdle that kept quite a few students from ever completing the degree.

My study applied a new intervention called "micro-counseling" to helping married partners improve their communication. The couples were taught active listening skills. We videotaped them before and after the training and found it was extremely effective. There's no way to know if the effect was long-lasting, but the basic dynamic underlies most marital counseling.

For me, the applications were endless in this new job, beginning with my first project—providing a communications skills training workshop to our rehab counselors through the CCE. We eventually had other training programs, but this one was the bedrock. We had a great program, and I had a perfect job for over ten years. Eventually, the grant ran out, but it was a wonderful position and returned countless dividends, especially in friendships. The CCE was where I met Mike Flynn and his wife, Casey, then their good friends Scott and Maryjo. They all became our closest and most valued friends for over thirty years—long after the old CCE had run its course.

Midway through this period, Nelson Otto (the director, always in pursuit of something new) left the program, and I was named to replace him. To be honest, I was thrilled to be in charge. That also meant I was now the guy to travel and represent the program regionally and nationally. Because the program still resided within the larger agency, I was also made a vice president of the MRC. A decent resume was developing, without a lot of effort on my part (or so it felt).

Thus began my twenty-year training career, born from my doctoral dissertation on communication skills training. I created a two-day workshop, where I taught the participants basic active listening skills. I videotaped them, then coached them on how to improve—*voilà!* This little gig would take me throughout the United States, to Western Europe, and beyond. It had our family living part of the year in a little town southwest of London, where we were provided a house. Our girls were enrolled in the English public school during their fourth-grade year.

Having never traveled outside the U.S., sitting in an English pub with a pint of bitter was a moment I truly savored. The experience also led to family trips to Ireland and France and a jaunt for me to South Africa. Such lifelong reference points these adventures provided. Whenever someone mentions French food, we think of a little corner café in Paris and the delectable sensation of eating scallops in a cream sauce. I was astonished by it, which was surprising for someone never very interested in food.

Not bad for a short phone call to John's cousin, Nancy, to whom I owe abundant gratitude.

25

Life Takes a Bad Turn

One winter morning—on our return from a visit to Jean's brother, Jon, and his wife in South Dakota—we encountered a gradually worsening snowstorm. We were driving our three-week-old, very subcompact Dodge Colt. As we neared St. James, Minnesota, our car slid sideways into the path of an oncoming semitruck. We crashed head on.

Jean was gravely injured, with her face smashed in and broken bones in her upper and lower limbs. She was taken by ambulance to the hospital in St. James, where they quickly determined her condition was critical. She had to be taken by another ambulance to a larger hospital, the nearest one being in Mankato, Minnesota.

Our car was completely demolished. My injuries were less serious, as the impact of the crash was more to the front and passenger side of the car. I had several broken ribs and other bruising, so I was also taken to the hospital in St. James. I remained there for several days of recovery; I was visited by my parents and, separately, by Jean's mom, Borgie, who was widowed by that time. There is one memorable anecdote of Borgie's visit (and it's among the countless reasons I loved her). When I confessed I'd been unable to urinate since my catheter had been removed, she went and got a pan of warm water, placed my hands in it, and … success!

26

our Miraculous Daughters

Once Jean was beyond her critical phase, she was transferred to the University of Minnesota's hospital for three more months of recovery and rehabilitation. She was eventually discharged home, but she still had to use crutches. And she was still using these crutches when the call came from the Wisconsin state adoption agency, where we'd been on the waiting list for over seven years.

They had a situation to discuss with us: a mother had given birth to *twins*, and we were next up. The agency had not had this situation before in their history, and they wanted us to *think about it*. The red-haired twin girls had an uncanny appearance that would fit perfectly into our family. The agency really preferred to place the girls together. (Can anyone conceive of Jessalyn and Bretta being placed *separately*?)

You can imagine how long we "thought about it."

After our joyous acceptance, we were scheduled to pick up the twins as soon as possible. They had been born at a hospital in Eau Claire, Wisconsin, and had gone to a temporary foster home about an hour from Hudson.

That Friday, Bretta and Jessie became our life. When the nurse placed them in the twin child seats in the back of our little Fiat, he said, "Well, your life will never be the same again."

Truer words…

When we arrived back in Hudson, we immediately called Jean's mom (who was living in Hudson at this point and was well aware of our mission to Eau Claire). We told her to come right over. When she came in, she stood in our entryway, and Jean came out and handed her the bundle containing *one* baby girl (which was all she knew about). After a few short moments, I came out carrying the other twin.

Borgie collapsed to the floor. How special the twins would be in her life—and oh, how immeasurably special she would be in theirs.

27

The River Trip

In hindsight, the timing seems suspect at best. John and I had long dreamt of and planned a trip down the Mississippi River—Tom Sawyer-style—but Jean was home alone, still on crutches from the car accident. Looking back, "arrested development" was perhaps the kindest thing you could say about me. But Jean (stubborn Norwegian) was fiercely independent and always ready to prove it. She said we should go ahead with our long-planned trip—her mom would stay with her to help out. Nothing to worry about.

It didn't turn out that way. First, it happened that Jean and I had been raising six ducklings, and they were close to being adults at the time. We'd given them silly names—Mu Shu Duck, Peking Duck, Moo Goo Gai Duck—and they were adorable. We kept them in an eight-foot-square corral that I'd made from chicken wire. One night, soon after John and I had left, a fox broke through the fencing and killed all the ducks.

A few more days into her *"I'll be fine alone"* adventure, a bat got in through the chimney. It flew madly around the house as she chased it. She was still hobbling on crutches, holding a blanket over her head with one hand and a broom in the other, trying desperately to get the critter out of the house. Finally, she reluctantly called for help. Her mother had a new fiancé, who was a retired veteran with thirty-four years of service. He'd been a gunner in the U.S. Navy, and he was the perfect man for the job. He came to her rescue and got the bat out.

Meanwhile, floating peacefully down the Mississippi River, John and I were without a care in the world. John had a small fifteen-foot run-about with a fifty-horsepower motor. We'd experimented with it on the St. Croix River. As the saying goes, what could possibly go wrong?

So we planned and took off on our trip—destination: St. Louis, Missouri. Our only cares were watching the boat's gas level and making sure there was enough beer and ice in the cooler.

Catastrophe, however, was not far from reach. Shortly after pulling out of Hudson—thankfully, just out of sight of the well-wishers—our motor stopped and would not restart. We began the laborious task of unpacking the entire back end of the boat so we could get to the dead motor. With amazing good luck, we found a carburetor linkage had become disconnected. We hooked it back up and were on our jolly (and very relieved) way.

Each day, in the late afternoon, we looked for a decent area to camp along the shoreline, ensuring we'd have enough time to set up our tent and find firewood. On one memorable night, we had a hard time finding a campsite and finally pulled ashore in the dark, pitching our tent near the front of the boat. We had just settled in when a stranger approached us. He'd come to warn us that some young guys had their eye on us and were planning to give us trouble in the middle of the night. We did not require any coaxing to pack up and get the hell out of there. We traveled a few miles down the river—a very treacherous thing to undertake in the pitch-black night on the river. Luckily, we came upon a small marina that, although closed for the night, offered lights and buildings and gave us some sense of safety. We set up camp nearby. We had felt genuine fear, and the experience put a noticeable dent in our happy-go-lucky adventure. But after a few beers, our bravery returned and we vowed to continue.

On another occasion, we awoke in the morning and, peering out of our tent, saw one of our gas tanks floating in the river, tethered to the boat by the fuel line. What was worse, this problem had been caused by our boat flooding and being pushed up onto the shore, likely by the wake of a passing barge. Not only was our boat parked on land, all our clothes and supplies were drenched. After a herculean effort to bail out the boat and carry it to the river, we spent the rest of the day at the laundromat in the next town.

On about the seventh day, we reached East Dubuque, Illinois, a small town just across the river from Dubuque, Iowa. The nightlife was a bit beyond what its parent city in Iowa would tolerate. Our youthful spirits were on a crusade to explore the *adult* world, so it was perfect. Late that night, we stumbled back to our camp, our heads swirling with images and memories we would long cherish.

28

Riverside Drive

Back in Hudson, Jean and I decided it was time to find a new home. This time, we really struck gold. Riverside Drive is a beautiful, winding road along the Willow River. It is also on Lake Mallalieu, which is formed by a dam where the river enters the St. Croix. We found a small yellow house with almost no windows and a rundown unattached garage. But it had over a hundred feet of lakefront. We loved it—and after a quick back and forth with the agent, we bought it for $67,000. We were extending a bit financially, but I was doing well, we didn't have the twins yet, and we thought, *Why not?* We so loved the place that late one night, after the purchase but before closing, we went there and sat on the dock, dreaming of our new life. A picture of nine-year-old Tara, posing on the dock, tells the whole story.

Yet more disaster loomed. We were at Jean's mom's when we got a call from the real estate agent. We'd lost the house. A previous bidder had come through after removing a financing contingency, and they had to accept his offer. We were devastated. After imagining life on the lake, looking elsewhere seemed impossible—but we had no choice.

After numerous disappointing visits, we had narrowed our search down to two properties—one with a distant view of Lake Mallalieu and one on the bluff overlooking the St. Croix River. We weren't thrilled about either, especially when we added in the small detail that these were only *properties*. We'd have to build a house. So we thought of staying put. I had added a big second-floor deck to our house, and we had a decent view of the St. Croix. But we were right downtown, and the night noise when the bars let out was more than we could tolerate.

One night, Jean's mom, who had shared every step of our plight, joined us out in her big backyard to drown our sorrows. That's where we were when the now-legendary call came—the other buyer's financing had fallen through, and the house was ours. Our rollercoaster life had crested. Our joy was overwhelming.

The dream had finally come true. Our life on Riverside Drive would become almost delirious in its beauty, joys, and richness. Lifelong friendships began here, and our wonderful twin daughters soon arrived. It was the home where we saw new life take hold and old lives end. We experienced the passing of our parents and felt the joy and the suffering of raising our children, then having to let them go—first to grade school (probably the hardest), then to college, and then to their lives as young adults.

This house was also a place where our old friends gathered and continued to be in our lives. Our love for Scott and Maryjo continued to thrive, and they came to enjoy the lake as much as we did. I will sometimes mention that I consider Scott my best friend, and this always brings the question: *What about John?*

I always answer that John is more than a friend. We have been close for so many years that I think of him as a brother. We understand each other in important, complex ways, and we can be very direct. When I look to John for support, I am sometimes only met with, "Well, I'm afraid I agree with Jean." Our early experiences predate us meeting either of our wives, but when they entered the picture, we were the best man in each other's weddings. Our wives became friends and even worked together for several years.

It's not without rough edges. When Dianne is critical of John, I rush to his defense. When John bends in humble deference to her, I coax him to resist. Then Jean weighs in, muddying her own relationships, especially with Dianne. Thus, we stumble along the rumpled fabric of our years together.

Riverside Drive came to be so many things. It was the port from which John and I embarked on our infamous ten-day adventure down the Mississippi River. Tara was thirteen when we bought the house, and she learned to water-ski on Lake Mallalieu. It was a neighborhood where new relationships entered our lives, blending into the moving current of our past. Initially, we were the "new young couple," but we later evolved to being "the older couple." The new and slightly younger folks accepted us, and we gradually transformed from a community of friendly neighbors into a close and supportive group of friends. Nothing is more rewarding than pulling into our driveway at night and finding one or two couples sitting in the garage at the Corner Bar and Counseling Center.

29

Settling into Paradise

Our home on Riverside Drive has been the gravity point of our family for forty years. It's where new babies had their toes dipped in lake water and where they later brought their friends for moonlight cruises. It's where the fourth Corner Bar and Counseling Center came into being (and still exists today).

Riverside Drive is like bubble wrap for the brain. I think our friends feel the same—you turn onto Riverside, coast down that big hill, follow the winding, narrow road along the river, and you arrive in paradise. "Lower Riverside," once a few fishing cabins, has evolved into a landscape of beautiful lakeside homes—a restful retreat from the city. Yet, as much as we treasure the bucolic setting, the real value is the community of friends. It's hard to imagine now that Jean and I were only about thirty years old—our marriage less than ten—when we settled into a place we would never leave.

Almost immediately, my mother bought us a pontoon boat. True to her nature, she just knew we should have one, and somehow she found an old one for six hundred dollars. John and I picked it up, and it was soon launched onto Lake Mallalieu.

A great era of stories and memories was launched along with it. I built a corrugated plastic roof for it, added twelve-volt amber lights under that roof, and (of course) added a bar. For all practical purposes, this was Corner Bar and Counseling Center number five. We installed a radio, speakers, and a toilet. Evening cruises were perfect for conversation and music, under the soft glow of amber lights.

The lake became our extended front yard, and we couldn't wait to head out on any occasion, especially happy hour. I would load up the cooler, Jean would make snacks, and out we would go, very often with our dear friends, Scott and Maryjo. But even when, or especially when, it was just Jean and me, we could cruise out at a moment's notice, without any driving or boat-hauling or the other drudgery usually involved in "going to the lake." Sunset cruises quickly became our favorite. This most beautiful time of day, coinciding with happy hour, provided the perfect daily ritual for reflecting on our day and watching the sunset.

On one memorable cruise, we had an uninvited passenger. Our neighbors next door had a little daughter named Addie, who was born just after they moved in. I adored her, owing in some part to the residual loss I carried from so many years before. On this occasion, I had invited all my office friends for an afternoon boat ride. We had loaded everything and were ready to shove off when, scampering madly across the yard, came little four-year-old Addie. She ran to the dock, jumped onto the boat, crawled up onto my lap, and put her head on my shoulder, where she slept the entire trip. I never did know what my work friends thought.

In later years, we always had our little girls along. They were born about the time we moved to the lake, so it was the only life they ever knew. (Doesn't everyone just go out on their boat every day?) But Jean and I knew we were living in heaven. It was also the perfect place to invite friends. One such visit, when John and Dianne drove over from St. Paul, proved auspicious.

We were sitting in our house, by our north-facing windows that overlook the neighbor's house. It had just gone up for sale. John and Dianne had been thinking about moving, and meticulous John had along his trusty yellow legal pad, on which he'd listed about twenty-five requirements for their next house. The last item read "preferably on the water."

The rest is history. In addition to living with the love of my life and the children we adored in the house of our dreams, I was about to have my best friend living next door. It was all hard to believe, but it turned out as great as expected. The stars had really lined up.

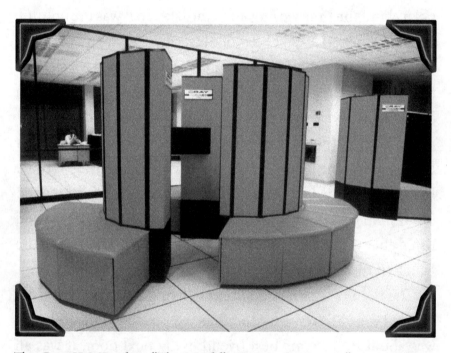

The Cray X-MP, a.k.a. "The World's Fastest Computer," circa 1982.

Courtesy of the National Center for Supercomputing Applications (NCSA) and the Board of Trustees of the University of Illinois.

30

Traveling at 14 Billion Words Per Second

As I mentioned in an earlier chapter, my graduate school dissertation was on applying communication skills training to help married couples improve their relationships. I would first videotape them through one-way glass as they interacted over some topic I provided. Then I'd teach them a series of active listening skills, followed by a second videotaped interaction. When trained observers compared the two sessions, the results were remarkable—and statistically significant. People could be quickly taught better communication. From this seed grew a career spanning decades and continents. The hallmark of my career became known as "account planning," which was first widely implemented during my time at Cray Research.

I had done essentially the same thing in my job at CCE, where we trained counselors for the U.S. Department of Vocational Rehab. Following that job, I was lucky to land the job at Cray. The position was in Human Resources, and I was responsible for employee training. Naturally, I introduced my communication skills training and began offering it as a workshop for field personnel. That process soon migrated to using these training sessions to focus on improving our relationships with key customers. When management caught wind of what I was doing with sales teams, they moved me into marketing, reporting to the VP of sales—an incredible move for a guy from (lowly) HR. I was off to the races.

The account planning process involved getting a team together to focus on one particular customer, such as Ford, the CIA, or Boeing. A team was typically a group of eight to twelve people, and my job was to facilitate their discussions. We would identify our major goals for the account; the goals would be substantial and far-reaching, such as, "Grow account revenue to $25 million in the next two years." Then we'd develop a plan to achieve it.

My role was to listen intently to everything that was said—like any good active listener—and feed it back to the team. I wrote everything on a flip chart, taping the pages around the room as they accumulated. The group came to understand and appreciate the role I was playing, and at the end of the usually two-day project, I would always get applause—sometimes a standing ovation. Then I would roll up all the messy chart pages, take them home, and convert them into an impressive-looking account plan, which I would email to the team. This final document was welcomed by the account manager, who felt he or she now had a plan with the buy-in of the whole team. Management loved it too. Local management was happy to have a plan they could use as a guide for building the account, and senior management was delirious.

I received the Excellence in Leadership Award one year, and I was called in to meet with the vice president of sales. He expressed his appreciation for what I was doing, and he suggested account planning should be done with all Cray accounts ... *worldwide.* He said the company would fly me back and forth to conduct the sessions; I suggested the efficiency of my moving to the European headquarters in England and working out of that base. One of my better suggestions.

I especially remember the intrigue of doing account planning sessions for "secret" government entities, like the NSA. No one was ever supposed to say the name of the entity ... *or even the initials.* Talk about cloak and dagger! There were other classified sites where, whenever certain topics came up, about half the room had to go into a completely secure special room. They would finish the discussion, then rejoin the rest of us ordinary people without clearances.

In addition to the NSA, we covered other top-secret sites, including:
- NDI (Navy Defense Intelligence)
- ARL (Army Research Lab, which is located outside of Baltimore and is where they design ballistics)
- Los Alamos (where they invented the atom bomb and have a terrific and horrifying museum about it)

- Navy Research Lab
- CIA
- NERSC (National Energy Research Center, "energy" meaning fusion)

These were all amazing experiences and windows into the world that few people get to see.

Very few outsiders get to spend time at Cray Research itself, in Chippewa Falls, Wisconsin. This is where Seymour Cray invented supercomputing and his team designed (among many things) the case that would contain the first Apple computer.

At Cray, the commercial side had slightly less intrigue, but it was still fascinating to know that products ranging from a Harley-Davidson Roadster to the Boeing DC-10 were designed on early Cray machines. Cars ranging from the Ford Taurus to the Nissan 300ZX owe both their visual design and engine performance to Cray. You can look around any day and see things that got the way they are with a touch of Cray supercomputing.

Today, Cray exascale supercomputing is operating in the cloud. It is run by Hewlett-Packard and tackles the massive new data requirements of problems ranging from artificial intelligence to the search for solutions to COVID-19.

I still feel thankful and honored to have met Seymour Cray. His untimely death at age seventy-one in 1996 left unanswered the question of what he may have accomplished with the new Cray Computer Company, which he was just establishing.

31

our Cloudy Life in England

One sunny morning in 1996, I was walking from the parking lot into work at Cray Research when I met a friend from the office. We chatted briefly. He was a bit senior to me in the business, a guy I respected. We were chatting amiably, or so it seemed to me, when he said rather abruptly, "Well, Gary, I have to go."

My first thought was, *Oh-oh...*

Then the sensations came ... not powerfully, but in a slow, distinct wave. It was as if someone dumped a noxious fluid into my brain and it was seeping down into my body. I felt nauseous. Gagging was a relief, but only momentarily. Quickly, the nausea returned. The discomfort traveled into my arms and legs, then out to the tips of my fingers and toes, making them tingle. The muscles in my lower legs grew painfully restless. It helped to walk, but as soon as I stopped walking, the muscle aches returned.

This weird concoction of symptoms added up to one thing. I'd had it before and I now knew what it was: depression. There was usually a trigger event, even something as innocuous as a friend saying he "had to get going," which I interpreted as rejection. That's all it took. I think this episode lasted about a year. I have a distinct and unpleasant memory of still struggling with it around 1997, when I was giving the girls their first driving lessons.

Another cloudy episode had occurred earlier during my account planning travels, just after Cray's decision to temporarily relocate me to work in Europe.

That fall, Jean and I and our two girls moved to England. The company rented us a house in the small village of Warfield, near Bracknell, where Cray had its European headquarters. As the British would say, it was "brilliant." The girls were nine at the time, and we enrolled them in the public school. They wore the traditional English schoolgirl uniform of knee-length stockings, gray skirts, and light blue blouses. They were quite the picture, especially as identical twins.

My work had me traveling to every country in Western Europe. The office would issue me a plane ticket and expense money in the local currency, then away I would go. It included a trip in South Africa, where a friend I'd worked with back in the U.S. at Cray happened to be stationed. He and I took a safari into the countryside north of Johannesburg. Other work trips took me to Paris, Munich, Amsterdam, Stockholm, Milan,

Copenhagen, and Maui. If not for the photos, I'd have a hard time believing all this happened. I once got lost looking for my hotel in Hannover, Germany. Being adrift in the dark, in a country where I didn't speak the language, was daunting. When I finally decided I'd better get help, I took a random exit off the freeway, drove into the city, and pulled over to ask directions. Then I discovered I had pulled up in front of the hotel! Jean must have been praying for me.

Despite the considerable stress and anxiety that always stuck with me, these were great experiences, and nearly always they were considered quite successful. However, I can also recount a failure or two.

One notable collapse was in Milan, where we were doing a session for an Italian automaker. I could not gain control of the group or of the account manager. They saw my program as an edict from HQ (and it was); they had no interest. I will never forget the evening between days one and two when, as was typical, the team went to dinner. I was stressed and exhausted. After a long, late-night dinner (where I had to feign eating), we sat around into the wee hours. Naturally, all of them were speaking their native Italian, and they were also smoking cigars. I still think of this evening as one of the lowest points of my life. My stomach ached. I did not sleep that night, and I had to be up early to lead the group on day two.

Despite these troubles, the good memories prevail. After the trauma of the Milan trip, I remember being back home in

Warfield and sitting at a table in the local pub. I was by the fireplace, under the low ceiling, with a pint of bitter. The perfect caption would have been, "Savoring the moment."

In England, we were provided a car—a turbo-charged Volvo sedan—which *proved* I was dreaming. On weekends, we explored Cornwall down to the southwest and as far north as Scotland. We also took a week vacation in Normandy, France. In all, it was a fantastic experience for our family, even when you include the fact I was generally depressed the entire time we lived there. I carried it with me and didn't tell anyone, not even Jean.

For Bretta and Jessie, this adventure was life-changing. They will forever be fond of England. They've each gone back as adults, and they remain in contact with Michelle, a neighbor girl their age from Warfield. We keep in touch with her parents, and Michelle has been here, cruising around with us on Lake Mallalieu.

Yet whatever I did, the dark clouds hung with me. Eventually, I shared these experiences with my family doctor during an otherwise routine visit. He took keen interest and suggested I consider taking an antidepressant. That sounded scary and like overkill to me. He said, "I don't think you will take them, but I think you should."

What could it hurt? I decided to give the pills a try; the prescription was for Paroxetine. I knew my pharmacist, Mark, and considered him a friend. He said I probably wouldn't feel anything for about two weeks. In one week, the darkness was gone. It was the best I had felt in twenty years, and it has never changed. I had my life back. One time, years later, I asked Mark if he thought I could discontinue these meds. His replied with no hesitation, "Oh, it will just come right back." I decided to continue.

Our family will always appreciate and treasure the experience of living in England. Back home in the U.S., when we sit at red lights, waiting an interminable length of time for them to change to green, we so miss the quick trips through stop-free roundabouts; when we drive through our typical suburbs—with old tires, rusted-out pickups, and dead lawn mowers resting around the properties—we miss the stark cleanliness of every English neighborhood. It is a beautiful country. God save the Queen.

32

Taking Chances and Letting Go

Raising our little girls on Riverside Drive was paradise for all of us. Naturally, as far as they knew, this was how everyone lived—afternoon boat rides, evening sunsets, and falling asleep to Dad reading books. When the girls reached the age of five, Jean and I dropped them off at the bus stop up the road and watched them head off to school. We were both surprised to find ourselves choked up on our walk back home. Would they be okay?

They would, of course, but the letting go was tough. The local public school system was among the best in the country, and they thrived in every way—top grades, musical talent, sports, and an abundance of friends. The band director, Chris, was phenomenal. But graduation came too quickly, and we were soon faced with another more serious parting—moving away from home for college. Once again, we were driving down the road to a separation that nobody wanted. And again, with teary eyes, we wished them good luck and waved goodbye, not quite feeling sure it was the right thing to do.

For Bretta and Jessie, college presented a unique and historic juncture, as they had chosen *separate schools* and would live apart from each other for the first time in their young lives.

Thanks in large part to their outstanding high school experience, college was a breeze. They both continued on to graduate school, each earning doctoral degrees—Jessie in nursing and Bretta in law, following in the footsteps of her older sister, Tara, who had earned a law degree a few years earlier. And when school was finally behind them, all three girls decided to live back in their home area, either because of (or in spite of) it being close to their loving parents. Having them still with us, in their adult lives, is quite a gift!

In the end, everything has settled down. Jean and I are at home together, where for over forty years we've been loving our life, loving each other, and watching the glorious, reflected sunset as it sweeps across the wooded eastern shore of our beautiful lake. Just where we belong.

For life.

Acknowledgments

Of the many people who helped me with this book, one person is foremost: Evonne Agnello, author of *Shaking Shame from Mental Illness*, published by Book Publishers Network in 2012. She generously shared her skill, experience, and insight. Her encouragement and gentle criticism helped make this book possible.

My parents provided me with a life that made for a good story, while my sisters, especially Janelle, added fabric and richness to our experiences. Later, my three fabulous daughters—Jessie, Bretta, and Tara—kept me going with their love, understanding, and occasional (but oh-so-welcome) requests for help from Dad. Bretta's patient help with this book has been invaluable.

And I must acknowledge the importance of my friendship with my best friend, John Halloran. Even the notion of having a true, lifelong friendship is exceptional. Ours has been legendary.

My greatest honor and gratitude go to my wife, Jean, who has certainly earned them.

References

Br. Paul-Vincent Niebauer, OSB, "Saint John's Abbey and University Church Bell Banner," 2017. Used with permission from the photographer.

Charles Levy, "Atomic Cloud Rises Over Nagasaki, Japan," 1945. Public domain, via Wikimedia Commons.

Guy de Maupassant, "A Piece of String." First published by Victor-Harvard, Cambridge, MA, in *Miss Harriet – A Short Story Collection*, 1884.

Hewlett Packard Enterprise. "High Performance Computing/ The Next Era of Supercomputing." https://www.hpe.com/us/en/compute/hpc/supercomputing/cray-exascale-super-computer.html. Available online: 2022, March 25.

Janelle Hill, "Academy of Holy Angels," 2021.

National Center for Supercomputing Applications (NCSA) and the Board of Trustees of the University of Illinois, "A Cray Supercomputer."

Pierce County Historical Association Photo Collection, "Street Scene – East Ellsworth – Wis."

Susan Halloran, "CA State Highway 9," 2022.

William Cullen Bryant, "Thanatopsis." First published by *The North American Review*, Boston, MA, 1815.

About the Author

This book is itself, of course, an autobiography. Gary and his wife, Jean, are still enjoying every sunset across beautiful Lake Mallalieu and cherishing the friendships that make up life on Riverside Drive.

CPSIA information can be obtained
at www.ICGtesting.com
Printed in the USA
JSHW050941150123
36207JS00006B/128